Custom Edition

Lab Manual
for *Starting Out with Programming Logic & Design*

Tony Gaddis

Taken from:

Lab Manual for Starting Out with Programming Logic & Design
by Tony Gaddis

Custom Publishing

New York   Boston   San Francisco
London   Toronto   Sydney   Tokyo   Singapore   Madrid
Mexico City   Munich   Paris   Cape Town   Hong Kong   Montreal

2008820062

KW

Pearson
Custom Publishing
is a division of

www.pearsonhighered.com

ISBN 10: 0-555-01528-9
ISBN 13: 978-0-555-01528-5

Table of Contents

Lab 1: Input, Processing, and Output.. **1**
    Lab 1.1 – Algorithms 1
    Lab 1.2 – Pseudocode 3
    Lab 1.3 – Flowcharts... 7
    Lab 1.4 – Python Code... 11
    Lab 1.5 – Programming Challenge 1: Team Average...................... 15
    Lab 1.6 – Programming Challenge 2: Pedometer Calculator 17

Lab 2: Modules.. **19**
    Lab 2.1 – Algorithms 19
    Lab 2.2 – Pseudocode and Modules..................................... 21
    Lab 2.3 – Flowcharts... 25
    Lab 2.4 – Python Code and Functions................................... 29
    Lab 2.5 – Python Code and Variables................................... 33
    Lab 2.6 – Writing a Complete Program 37
    Lab 2.7 – Programming Challenge 1: Retail Tax 41

Lab 3: Decisions and Boolean Logic I... **43**
    Lab 3.1 – Evaluating Conditions... 43
    Lab 3.2 – Pseudocode and Decisions................................... 45
    Lab 3.3 – Flowcharts... 47
    Lab 3.4 – Python Code... 51
    Lab 3.5 – Programming Challenge 1: Guess the Secrets 55

Lab 4: Decisions and Boolean Logic II.. **57**
    Lab 4.1 – Logical Operators and Dual Alternative Decisions 57
    Lab 4.2 – Pseudocode: Dual Alternative Decisions........................ 59
    Lab 4.3 – Pseudocode: Nested Decision Structures........................ 63
    Lab 4.4 – Flowcharts... 67
    Lab 4.5 – Python Code... 73
    Lab 4.6 – Programming Challenge 1: Tip, Tax, and Total 77

Lab 5: Repetition Structures I **79**
    Lab 5.1 – Repetition Structures Pseudocode:
        Condition-Controlled Loops 79
    Lab 5.2 – Repetition Structures Pseudocode:
        Counter-Controlled Loops 83
    Lab 5.3 – Flowcharts... 87
    Lab 5.4 – Python Code... 93
    Lab 5.5 – Programming Challenge 1: Yum Yum Burger Joint 97

Lab 6: Repetition Structures II **99**
    Lab 6.1 – For Loop and Pseudocode.................................. 99
    Lab 6.2 – For Loop and Flowcharts 103
    Lab 6.3 – Python Code.. 109
    Lab 6.4 – Programming Challenge 1: Average Test Scores 115

Lab 7: Functions.. **117**
    Lab 7.1 – Functions and Pseudocode................................ 117
    Lab 7.2 – Functions and Flowcharts 121
    Lab 7.3 – Python Code and Random 125
    Lab 7.4 – Python Code and Formatting 129
    Lab 7.5 – Programming Challenge 1: Math Problems.................... 131

Lab 8: Input Validation **133**
    Lab 8.1 – Input Validation 133
    Lab 8.2 – Input Validation and Pseudocode 135
    Lab 8.3 – Functions and Flowcharts 139
    Lab 8.4 – Python Code and Input Validation.................. 143
    Lab 8.5 – Programming Challenge 1: Cell Phone
            Minute Calculator... 145

Lab 9: Arrays... **149**
    Lab 9.1 – Arrays and Pseudocode.................................... 149
    Lab 9.2 – Checking the Work 155
    Lab 9.3 – Arrays and Flowcharts 157
    Lab 9.4 – Arrays and Python Code 161
    Lab 9.5 – Programming Challenge 1: Going Green 167

Lab 10: File Access.. **171**
    Lab 10.1 – File Access and Pseudocode 171
    Lab 10.2 – File Access and Flowchart............................. 177
    Lab 10.3 – File Access and Python Code 183
    Lab 10.4 – Programming Challenge 1: Going Green
            and File Interaction 189

Lab 1: Input, Processing, and Output
This lab accompanies Chapter 2 of *Starting Out with Programming Logic & Design.*

Name: _____

Lab 1.1 – Algorithms

Critical Review

An **algorithm** is a set of well-designed, logical steps that must take place in order to solve a problem.

The algorithm's flow is *sequential*. For example, before you process calculations, all needed data must be retrieved.

This lab requires you to think about the steps that takes place in a program by writing algorithms. Read the following problem prior to completing the lab.

> Write a program that will take in basic information from a student: student name, degree name, how many credits they have taken so far, and the total number of credits required in the degree program. The program will then calculate how many credits are needed to graduate. Display should include the student name, the degree name, and credits left to graduate.

Step 1: Examine the following algorithm. (Reference Designing a Program, page 30).

1. Get the student name.
2. Get the degree program name.
3. Subtract the number of credits taken so far from the required credits for the degree.
4. Get the number of credits required for the degree program.
5. Get the number of credits the student has taken so far.
6. Display the input information in Step 1 and 2.
7. Display the calculated information.

Step 2: What logic error do you spot?

_____

_____

_____

Step 3: How would you write the algorithm to fix the logic error?

_____

_____

_____

_____

_____

_____

_____

Step 4: What steps require user interaction (Ex: user must type in some input)?

_____

_____

_____

Name: _____

Lab 1.2 – Pseudocode

Critical Review

Pseudocode is an informal language that has no syntax rules, and is not meant to be compiled or executed.

The program's flow is *sequential*. For example, before you ask for input, you should display what information you want from the user.

//**Comments** are done by putting two forward slashes before the lines you want
//to document. Comments are used to explain code.

Variables are named storage locations.

Declare is the keyword used before naming a variable. **Data types** are Real for decimal numbers, Integer for whole numbers, and String for a series of characters.

Follow the rules for naming variables:
(1) Must be one word, no spaces
(2) Usually no punctuation characters, only letters and numbers
(3) Name cannot start with a number

Display is the keyword used to print something to the screen. Put any information to be displayed to the user inside quotation marks, such as:
Display "This is how you print something to the screen."
When using Display to print both a string and the value of a variable, use a comma between them, such as:
Display "Here is the average", average

Input is the keyword used to get the user to enter data. The data value entered by the user will be placed in the variable that follows the keyword input, such as:
Input variableName

Set is the keyword used before a calculation. Standard math operators are used such as + - * / MOD ^. Operators can be combined in one calculation, but it is wise to group expressions together using parentheses. Remember the order of operations. Some examples are *Set sale = price – discount* and *Set average = (test1 + test2 + test3) / 3*.

This lab requires you to think about the steps that takes place in a program by writing pseudocode. Read the following problem prior to completing the lab.

Write a program that will take in basic information from a student: student name, degree name, how many credits they have so far, and the total number of credits required in the degree program. The program will then calculate how many credits are needed to graduate. Display should include the student name, the degree name, and credits left to graduate.

Step 1: This program is most easily solved using just five variables. Identify potential problems with the following variables declared in the pseudocode. (Reference Variable Names, pp. 39-40.)

Variable Name	Problem (Yes or No)	If Yes, what's wrong?
Declare Real creditsTaken		
Declare Real credits Degree		
Declare Int creditsLeft		
Declare Real studentName		
Declare String degreeName		

Step 2: Complete the pseudocode by writing the two missing lines. (Reference Prompting the User, p. 42).

```
Display "Enter student name."
_____

Display "Enter degree program."
Input degreeName
_____

Input creditsDegree
```

Step 3: What two things are wrong with the following calculation? (Reference Variable Assignment and Calculations, p. 43).

```
creditsLeft = creditsTaken - creditsDegree
```

_____

_____

Step 4: Write the exact output would you expect from the following line of code if the user of the program enters "Bill Jones." (Reference Displaying Items, pp. 40-41.)

```
Display "The student's name is ", studentName
```

_____

Step 5: Write the exact output would you expect from the following line of code if the user of the program enters a degree that is 63 credits in total and they have taken 40. (Reference Displaying Items, pp. 40-41.)

```
Display "This program requires ", creditsDegree, "
credits and they have taken ",  creditsTaken, " so far."
```

_____

Step 6: Complete the following pseudocode to solve the programming problem.

```
1. //This program takes in student information and calculates
2. //how many credits the student has left before graduation.
3. //Information is then printed to the screen.

4. //Declare variables
```
5. _____
6. _____
7. _____
8. _____
9. _____

```
10.//Asks for user input
```
11._____
12._____
13._____
14._____
15._____
16._____
17._____
18._____

```
19.//Calculate remaining credits
```
20._____

```
21.//Display requested information - Student Name, Degree
22.//Program, and Credits Left.
23._____
24._____
25._____
```

Name: _____

Lab 1.3 – Flowcharts

Critical Review

A **flowchart** is a diagram that graphically depicts the steps that take place in a program. Symbols are used to depict the various steps that need to happen within a program. Flow lines are used between the symbols to indicate the flow of the program.

Ovals, the terminal symbol, are used as terminal symbols, which indicate a start and stop to a program.

Parallelograms, the data symbol, are used for input and display statements.

Rectangles, the process symbol, are used for calculations and variable declarations.

On page connectors are used to link a flowchart that continues on the same page. The connecting system starts with the letter A, whereas A would appear in the two connectors that show the flow.

The statements inside the data and the process symbols can be written similar to the statements used in pseudocode.

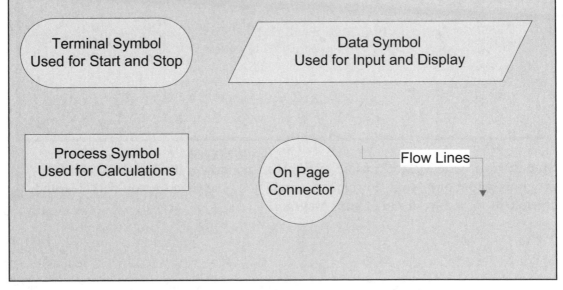

This lab requires you to think about the steps that take place in a program by designing a flowchart. While designing flowcharts can be done with paper and pencil, one mistake often requires a lot of erasing. Therefore, a flowcharting application such as Raptor or Visio should be used. This lab will give you a brief overview of Raptor. Read the following problem prior to completing the lab.

```
Write a program that will take in basic information from
a student including student name, degree name, how many
credits they taken so far, and the total number of
credits required in the degree program. The program will
then calculate how many credits are needed to graduate.
Display should include the student name, the degree
name, and credits left to graduate.
```

Step 1: Start Raptor and notice the Raptor screen. This window is your primary tool for creating a flowchart. Prior to adding symbols, save your document by clicking on File and then Save. Select your location and save the file as *Lab 1-3*. The *.rap* file extension will be added automatically.

Step 2: Notice the MasterConsole screen. This window is used to show your program output once your flowchart is completed. The Clear button will clear the console to view a fresh run of your program.

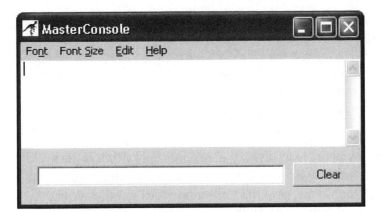

Step 3: Return to the Raptor screen to begin adding symbols into your flowchart. Your flowchart should follow the pseudocode in Lab 1-2, Step 6. While a rectangle is normally used for declaring variables, there is no easy way to do this in Raptor. Since this is an important part to flowcharting, we will do this using a comment box. To do this, Right-Click on the Start symbol and select Comment. In the Enter Comment box, type the variables your program will need. Below is a start to how it should look.

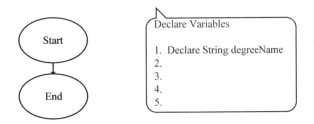

Step 4: The next step in your flowchart should be to ask for user input. Click the Input Symbol on the Left and Drag and Drop to the flow line between Start and Stop. Double Click on the Input Symbol to begin entering information. Enter `Enter student name` in the top box. Enter `studentName` in the variable box. Below is how it should look.

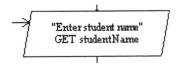

Step 5: Continue the Step 4 directions for all your input statements, changing each Input symbol to reflect the appropriate user interaction.

Step 6: The next step in your flowchart is to process any calculations that exist. Click on the Assignment symbol and drag it to the flow line between the last input statement and the end symbol. Double click on the Assignment symbol to enter your code. In the Set box, put the name of your storage variable. In the To box, put the expression part of your formula. Below is how it should look.

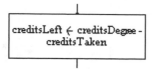

Step 7: The next step in your flowchart is to display the requested output to the screen. Click the Output symbol and drag it to the flow line between the assignment statement and the end symbol. Double click on the Output symbol to enter your code. Under Output Type, select Output Expression since we want to display both a sentence and the contents of a variable. In the box, type `"Student name is " + studentName`. Below is how it should look once you click Done.

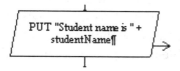

Step 8: Continue the Step 7 directions for all your output statements, changing each Output symbol to reflect the appropriate requested output information.

Step 9: Once your flowchart is complete, click on Run and then Execute to Completion on the Raptor menu. Follow the flow of your program to see if it processes properly. Your Master Console window should show output similar to

```
Student name is Bill Jones
The degree program is Computer Programming
Credits left to graduation is 39
----Run finished----
```

Step 10: The final step is to print out your finished flowchart and turn it in to your instructor. Inside Raptor, select File and the Print to Clipboard from the menu. Open Word, then select Edit and Paste to put your flowchart in a Word document. Save and print.

Name: _____

Lab 1.4 – Python Code

Critical Review

Comments in Python are preceded by the # sign.

Input of strings into a variable is done using the *raw_input* function. This function converts the input to a series of characters so they can be used later in the program. This is often written as an equation, such as:
  stringVariable = raw_input('Enter a word.')

Input of numeric values into a variable is done using the *input* function. The method of input is similar to string input. For example:
  realVariable = input("Enter a decimal value.')

Equations are written similarly to the method done in pseudocode without the *Set* keyword. For example,
  total = apples + oranges

Complex formulas should use parentheses to group processes. In addition, if input values are taken in as integers but will be used to calculate a decimal value, they must be converted to real values. For example:
  average = (test1 + test2) / 2

To display information to the screen, the ***print*** command is used with the string to be displayed written within single quotation marks. If you need to display the value of a variable after the string, separate the two by a comma. For example:
  print 'The average is', average

This lab requires you to translate your work in the pseudocode and flowchart to actual code using Python. Read the following problem prior to completing the lab.

```
Write a program that will take in basic information from
a student: student name, degree name, how many credits
they have taken so far, and the total number of credits
required in the degree program. The program will then
calculate how many credits are needed to graduate.
Display should include the student name, the degree
name, and credits left to graduate.
```

Step 1: Examine the following line of code. What do you expect as output to the screen?

```
studentName = raw_input('Enter student name. ')
```

_____

_____

Step 2: Examine the following line of code. What type of value do you expect the user to enter?

```
creditsDegree = input('Enter credits required for
degree.'
```

_____

_____

Step 3: Select (mark with an X) which function should be used to take in input from the user. The functions *raw_input* or *input* are determined based on the data type of the variable.

	raw_input( )	*input( )*
studentName	_____	_____
creditsDegree	_____	_____
creditsLeft	_____	_____

Step 4: If the user of the program types `Bill Jones` to the question in Step 1, what do you expect the output to the screen to be when the following line of code processes?

```
print 'The student\'s name is', studentName
```

_____

_____

Step 5: Examine the following line of code. If the program requires 63 credits, and the student has 20 left, what do you expect the output to the screen to be?

```
print 'The program requires', creditsDegree, 'credits
and they have taken', creditsTaken, 'credits so far.'
```

_____

_____

Step 6: Start the IDLE Environment for Python. If the Edit window for entering code does not come up, go to Options, Configure IDLE, click on the General tab, and under Startup Preferences select Open Edit Window. Close and reopen the Environment. Prior to entering code, save your file by clicking on File and then Save. Select your location and save this file as *Lab1-4.py*. Be sure to include the .py extension.

Step 7: Code should start with documentation. Document the first few lines of your program to include your name, the date, and a brief description of what the program does. Each line that you want to comment out must begin with a # sign. For example:

```
#Sally Smith
#January 15
#This program ...
```

Step 8: After documentation, enter the following line of code into your program.

```
studentName = raw_input('Enter student name. ')
```

Step 9: On the menu, select Run and then Run Module. Observe your program in action. If you get a syntax error, you must fix it before you are able to run your program. Click OK and review the highlighted syntax error to fix it.

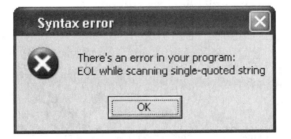

Step 10: Repeat Step 8, but change the statement so that it asks the user to enter the degree name. It is up to you whether you want to repeat Step 9 each time you code a line. It is recommended for beginning programmers so they can immediately identify syntax errors. Also, one syntax error at a time seems easier to handle than many all at once.

Step 11: Next, you should write the code that will ask the user how many credits are required in the degree. This can be done using the *input* function because it is a numeric value. Enter the following line of code into your program as a single line.

```
creditsDegree = input('Enter the number of credits
required for the degree. ')
```

Step 12: Repeat Step 11 but change the statement so that it asks the user to enter the number of credits they have so far.

Step 13: Next, add your calculation. This is done very simply with the following code.

```
creditsLeft = creditsDegree - creditsTaken
```

Step 14: Add the following line of code to your program.

```
print 'The student's name is', studentName
```

Step 15: If you have not tested your program in a while, now is a good time to try it out. Go to Run and Run Module and observe what happens. ***SYNTAX ERROR!***

Step 16: While nothing stands out as being wrong in Step 15, notice that the word `student's` is actually causing the problem. To the language, the apostrophe looks as if it is the end of the statement. Since it is not, it must be quoted out by putting a \ in front of it. Change the line to the following.

```
print 'The student\'s name is', studentName
```

Step 17: Finish your code by printing the remaining of the requested statements. Your final output might look like the following.

```
Enter student name. Bill Jones
Enter degree name. Computer Programming
Enter the number of credits required for the degree. 63
Enter the number of credits taken so far. 24

The student's name is Bill Jones
The degree name is Computer Programming
There are 39.0 credits left until graduation.
```

Step 18: When your code is complete and runs properly, on the Menu, go to Edit and then Select All, then Edit and Copy. Open Word and paste the code into a new Word document. Save and print. Turn in your code to your instructor.

Name: _____

Lab 1.5 – Programming Challenge 1: Team Average

For the following programming problem, write:
1. the algorithm
2. the pseudocode
3. the flowchart
4. Python code

Copy and paste your work into a Word document, labeling each section. Save and print your document, then turn it in for grading.

Team Average

A college wants you to write a program for them that will calculate the average number of wins for their football team over the past five years. The program user should be able to enter the number of wins each year. The program will calculate the average number of wins during that five year period and display that information to the screen.

Name: _____

Lab 1.6 – Programming Challenge 2: Pedometer Calculator

For the following programming problem, write:
1. the algorithm
2. the pseudocode
3. the flowchart
4. Python code

Copy and paste your work into a Word document, labeling each section. Save and print your document, then turn it in for grading.

Pedometer Calculator

A dietician wants you to write a program that will calculate the number of calories a person can use by walking at a slow pace for a mile. However, she only has the distance on the pedometer, which is measured in steps and not miles. Each mile a person walks equals 2000 steps. For every mile, a person uses 65 calories. Allow the program user to enter the number of steps taken throughout their day. The program will calculate the distance in miles and the number of calories used up. The user should also be able to enter the day of the week the data is being calculated for. The day of the week, the distance in miles, and the calories should then be displayed to the screen.

Lab 2: Modules
This lab accompanies Chapter 3 of *Starting Out with Programming Logic & Design*.

Name: _____

Lab 2.1 – Algorithms

This lab requires you to think about the steps that take place in a program by writing algorithms. Read the following problem before completing the lab.

> A retail company must file a monthly sales tax report listing the total sales for the month and the amount of state and county sales tax collected. The state sales tax rate is 4 percent and the county sales tax rate is 2 percent.
>
> Write a program that asks the user to enter the total sales for the month. The application should calculate and display the following:
> - The amount of county sales tax
> - The amount of state sales tax
> - The total sales tax (county plus state)

Step 1: Examine the following algorithm.

1. Get the total sales for the month.
2. Multiply the total sales by .04 to calculate the state sales tax.
3. Multiply the total sales by .02 to calculate the county sales tax.
4. Add the state tax and county tax to calculate the total sales tax.
5. Display the calculated county tax, state tax, and total sales tax.

Step 2: Given a total sales of $27,097, answer the following:

What is calculated the state tax? _____

What is the calculated county tax? _____

What is the calculated total tax? _____

Name: _____

Lab 2.2 – Pseudocode and Modules

Critical Review

A **module** is a group of statements that exist within a program for the purpose of performing a specific task.

Modules are commonly called procedures, subroutines, subprograms, methods, and functions.

The code for a module is known as a *module definition*. To execute the module, you write a statement that calls it.

The rules for naming modules are similar to those for naming variables.

The format for a module definition is as follows:

```
Module name( )
      Statement
      Statement
      Etc.
End Module
```

Calling a module is normally done from the Main ( ) module such as:

```
Call name( )
```

Generally, local variables should be used and arguments should be passed by reference when the value of the variable is changed in the module and needs to be retained. For example:

```
Module main( )
      Real Integer number
      Call inputData(number)
      Call printData(number)
End Module

//accepts number as a reference so the changed
// value will be retained
Module inputData(Real Ref number)
      Number = 20
End Module

//number does not to be sent as a reference
//because number is not going to be modified
Module printData(number)
      Display "The number is ", number
End Module
```

This lab requires you to think about the steps that take place in a program by writing pseudocode. Read the following program before completing the lab.

```
A retail company must file a monthly sales tax report
listing the total sales for the month and the amount of
state and county sales tax collected. The state sales
tax rate is 4 percent and the county sales tax rate is 2
percent.

Write a program that asks the user to enter the total
sales for the month. The application should calculate
and display the following:
```
   - The amount of county sales tax
   - The amount of state sales tax
   - The total sales tax (county plus state)

Step 1: This program is most easily solved using just four variables. Declare the variables that you will need in the program, using the proper data type and documenting the purpose.

Variable Name	Purpose
Declare Real totalSales	Stores total sales the user inputs

Step 2: Given the major task involved in this program, what modules might you consider including? List them and also describe the purpose of the module. (Reference Defining and Calling a Module, p. 78).

Module Name	Purpose
Module inputData ()	Allows the user to enter required user input

Step 3: Complete the pseudocode by writing the missing lines. (Reference Defining and Calling a Module, pp. 78-81). Also, when writing your modules and making calls, be sure to pass necessary variables as arguments and accept them as reference parameters if they need to be modified in the module. (Reference Passing Arguments by Value and by Reference, pp. 97-103).

```
Module main ()
      //Declare local variables
      Declare Real totalSales

      _____

      _____

      _____

      _____


      //Function calls
      Call inputData(totalSales)
      Call calcCounty(totalSales, countyTax)

      _____

      _____

      _____
End Module


//this module takes in the required user input
Module inputData(Real Ref totalSales)
      Display "Enter the total sales for the month."
      Input totalSales
End Module


//this module calculates county tax
//totalSales can be a value parameter because it is not
//changed in the module.
//countyTax must be a reference parameter because it is
//changed in the module
Module calcCounty(Real totalSales, Real Ref countyTax)
      countyTax = totalSales * .02
End Module


//this module calculates state tax

Module _____

      _____

      _____

      _____

      _____
End Module
```

```
//this module calculates total tax
Module _____

       _____

       _____

       _____

       _____

End Module

//this module prints the total, county, and state tax
Module _____

       _____

       _____

       _____

       _____

End Module
```

Name: _____

Lab 2.3 – Flowcharts

Critical Review

The flowchart symbol used for a **function call** is a rectangle with vertical bars on each side:

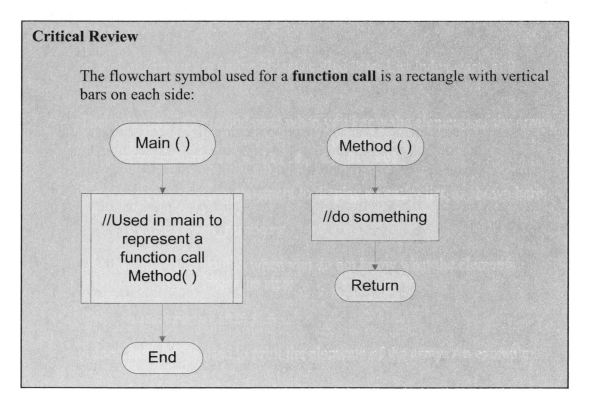

This lab requires you to think about the steps that take place in a program by designing a flowchart. Use an application such as Raptor or Visio. The instructions assume you are using Raptor. Read the following problem before completing the lab.

A retail company must file a monthly sales tax report listing the total sales for the month, and the amount of state and county sales tax collected. The state sales tax rate is 4 percent and the county sales tax rate is 2 percent.

Write a program that asks the user to enter the total sales for the month. The application should calculate and display the following:
- The amount of county sales tax
- The amount of state sales tax
- The total sales tax (county plus state)

Step 1: Start Raptor and save your document as *Lab 2-3*. The *.rap* file extension will be added automatically. Start by adding a Comment box that declares your variables. Here is a start to how your Comment box should look:

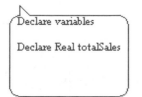

Step 2: The next step in your flowchart should be to call your methods. Click the Call Symbol on the Left and Drag and Drop to the flow lines between Start and Stop. Double click on the Call Symbol and type the name of your first method. For example, type *inputData* in the Enter Call box. Do not put the ( ) when using Raptor. Click the Done button. A new box will pop up that will ask you to create a new tab. Click Yes. A new tab will be created for your new method. Notice the new Tab called *inputData*.

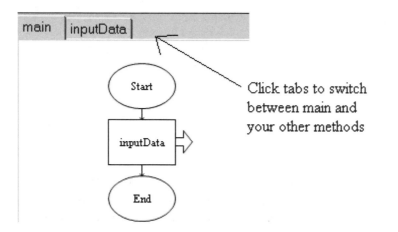

Step 3: Continue this process to add your additional methods, those being calcCounty() calcState(), calcTotal() and printData().

Step 4: Click on the inputData tab and add the necessary code as identified in your pseudocode in *Lab 2.2*. In Raptor, there is no need to pass variables as References as in pseudocode. Your inputData method might look like the following:

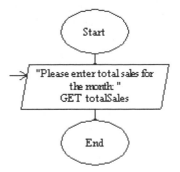

Step 5: Continue to code the remaining methods, those being calcCounty() calcState(), calcTotal() and printData(). If you happen to execute your program without completing your program, an error will occur such as:

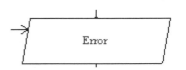

Your calculations methods input box might look like the following:

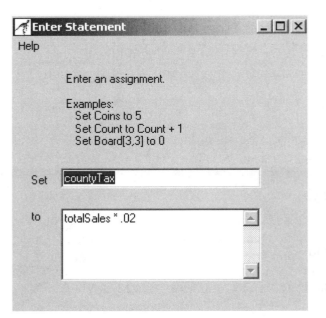

Your output data methods box might look like the following:

Step 6: After your program is complete, click Run then Execute to Finish. For your input, enter 67854 as your total monthly sales. If your program is coded correctly, the output should be as follows:

```
The county tax is $1357.0800
The state sales tax is $2714.1600
The total tax is $ 4071.2400
----Run finished----
```

Step 7: The final step is to print out your finished flowchart and turn it in to your instructor. Inside Raptor, select File and the Print to Clipboard from the menu. Open Word, then select Edit and Paste to put your flowchart in a Word document. Save and print.

Name: _____

Lab 2.4 – Python Code and Functions

> **Critical Review**
>
> The code for a function is known as a **function definition**. To execute the function, you write a statement that calls it.
>
> To create a function, you write its definition. The keyword *def* is used before a function name, followed by parentheses and a colon. Here is the general format of a function definition in Python:
>
> ```
> def function_name():
>     statement
>     statement
>     etc.
> ```
>
> Calling a function is done in order to make the module execute. The general format is:
>
> ```
> function_name()
> ```
>
> Function names must be flushed to the left.
>
> Statements within a module must be aligned evenly in order to avoid syntax errors.

Step 1: Start the IDLE Environment for Python. Prior to entering code, save your file by clicking on File and then Save. Select your location and save this file as *Lab2-4.py*. Be sure to include the .py extension.

Step 2: Document the first few lines of your program to include your name, the date, and a brief description of what the program does. Description of the program should be:

```
#This program will demonstrate various ways to
#use functions in Python.
```

Step 3: After your documentation, add the following function definition and function call:

```
#This function is to welcome people to my program
def welcome_message():
```

```
        print 'Welcome to my program using functions'
        print 'My name is Joe Student'

    #This is a function call
    welcome_message()
```

Step 4: Click Run, the Run Module to see your output. It should look like the following:

```
IDLE 1.2.1
>>> =================== RESTART
=====================
>>>
Welcome to my program using functions
My name is Joe Student
>>>
```

Step 5: Change your program so that the function call is tabbed over:

```
    #This function is to welcome people to my program
    def welcome_message():
        print 'Welcome to my program using functions'
        print 'My name is Joe Student'

    #This is a function call
        welcome_message()    #tab this line over
```

Step 6: Click Run and Run Module again. You'll notice that nothing is printed. This is because in Python, each line in a block must be indented and aligned. Function calls must be flushed to the left, and each line within a module must be aligned evenly. The following will cause a syntax error:

```
    def my_function():
        print 'And now for'
      print 'something completely'
       print 'different.'
```

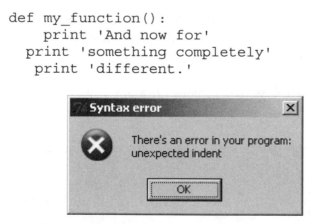

Step 7: Since programs normally center around a main function, modify your program so that it looks like this:

30

```
#The main function
def main():
    welcome_message()
    #causes welcome_message to run

#This function is to welcome people to my program
def welcome_message():
    print 'Welcome to my program using functions'
    print 'My name is Joe Student'

#This is the main function that starts the program
#in motion
main()    #calls main
```

Step 8: Add an additional function to your program that is called goodbye_message( ). The contents of this function should print a goodbye message. Execute your program so that it works then copy and paste your work into a Word document. Save and print your document, then turn it in for grading.

Name: _____

Lab 2.5 – Python Code and Variables

Critical Review

Variables can either be local or global in scope.

A local variable is created inside a function and cannot be accessed by statements that are outside a function, unless they are passed.

A local variable that needs to be used in multiple functions should be passed to the necessary functions.

An **argument** is any piece of data that is passed into a function when the function in called. A **parameter** is a variable that receives an argument that is passed into a function.

A global variable can be accessed by any function within the program, but should be avoided if at all possible.

Step 1: Start the IDLE Environment for Python. Prior to entering code, save your file by clicking on File and then Save. Select your location and save this file as *Lab2-5.py*. Be sure to include the .py extension.

Step 2: Document the first few lines of your program to include your name, the date, and a brief description of what the program does. Description of the program should be:

```
#This program demonstrates how to use variables and
#functions.
```

Step 3: Add a function called main( ) and a function call to main. Your code might look as follows:

```
#This program uses functions and variables

#the main function
def main():
    print 'Welcome to the tip calculator program'
    print   #prints a blank line

#calls main
main()
```

Step 4: Add a function called inputName() under the def main(): function. Your code might look as follows:

```
#this function inputs name
def inputName()
```

Step 5: Under your function definition, write a statement that allows the user to enter his or her name. Inside of the main function, call inputName() and write a print statement that displays the name. Your code might look like this:

```
#This program uses functions and variables

#the main function
def main():
    print 'Welcome to the variable program'
    print    #prints a blank line
    inputName()
    print 'Hello', name

#this function inputs name
def inputName():
    name = raw_input('Enter your name: ')

#calls main
main()
```

Step 6: Compile and run your program. Notice that when the program attempts to display the name, a syntax error occurs. This is because name is declared as a local variable within the inputName( ) function and main cannot access it.

Step 7: There are a couple of ways to fix this error. Examine the following code:

```
#This program uses functions and variables

#the main function
def main():
    print 'Welcome to the variable program'
    print    #prints a blank line

    name = inputName()
    print 'Hello', name

#this function inputs data
def inputName():
    name = raw_input('Enter your name: ')
    return name

#calls main
main()
```

The local variable name is declared in main and set equal to whatever the inputName( ) function returns. Notice the return name that is at the end of the inputName( ) function. This passes the value that was taken in back to main.

Step 8: Add an additional function to your program that is called inputAge( ). The contents of this function should be structured similarly to the inputName( ) function except that it asks the user to enter their age. Additionally, make a call to this new function such as age = inputAge( ). You should also display the value of age after the name is displayed.

Execute your program so that it works then copy and paste your work into a Word document. Save and print your document, then turn it in for grading.

Name: _____

Lab 2.6 – Writing a Complete Program

Step 1: Start the IDLE Environment for Python. Prior to entering code, save your file by clicking on File and then Save. Select your location and save this file as *Lab2-6.py*. Be sure to include the .py extension.

Step 2: Document the first few lines of your program to include your name, the date, and a brief description of what the program does. Use this for your description of the program:

> Write a program that will calculate a 20% tip and a 6% tax on a meal price. The user will enter the meal price and the program will calculate tip, tax, and the total. The total is the meal price plus the tip plus the tax.

Step 3: Add a function called main( ) and a function call to main.

Step 4: Add the function definition for input_meal( ), calc_tip( ), calc_tax( ), calc_total(), and print_info( ). Your code might look like the following:

```
#This program uses functions and variables

#the main function
def main():
    print 'Welcome to the meal calculator program'
    print   #prints a blank line

#this function will input meal price
def input_meal():

#this function will calculate tip at 20%
def calc_tip():

#this function will calculate tax at 6%
def calc_tax():

#this function will calculate tip, tax, and the
# total cost
def calc_total():

#this function will print tip, tax, the mealprice,
#and the total
def print_info():


#calls main
main()
```

Step 5: Inside of main() under the `print #prints a blank line` statement, create a local variable named mealprice that is set to the input_meal() function. This should look like the following:

```
mealprice = input_meal()
```

Step 6: Add the following lines of code inside of input_meal() function. This should look like the following:

```
mealprice = input('Enter the meal price $')
mealprice = float(mealprice)
return mealprice
```

The first line asks the user to enter the meal price. The second line converts the value to a float, since it will likely be a decimal value. This must be done with all potential decimal values that the user enters. The third line returns the input value of mealprice to the place where it was called (in Step 5).

Step 7: Inside of main() under the `meal = input_meal()` statement, create a local variable named tip that is set to the calc_tip() function. In this case, you must pass mealprice to the function, so it must be placed between the parentheses. This should look like the following:

```
tip = calc_tip(mealprice)
```

Step 8: Add the following lines of code inside of calc_tip(mealprice) function. The entire function should look like the following:

```
def calc_tip(mealprice):
        tip = mealprice * .20
        return tip
```

The first line is the function definition. It accepts mealprice as a parameter. The second line is to calculate tip as 20% of the mealprice. The third line returns the calculated tip to the place where it is called.

Step 9: Inside of main() under the `tip = calc_tip(mealprice)` statement, create a local variable named tax that is set to the calc_tax() function. In this case, you must pass mealprice to the function, so it must be placed between the parentheses. This should look like the following:

```
tax = calc_tax(mealprice)
```

Step 10: Add the following lines of code inside of calc_tax(mealprice) function. The entire function should look like the following:

```
def calc_tax(mealprice):
        tax = mealprice * .06
        return tax
```

The first line is the function definition. It accepts mealprice as a parameter. The second line is to calculate tax as 6% of the mealprice. The third line returns the calculated tax to the place where it is called.

Step 11: Inside of main() under the tax = calc_tax(mealprice) statement, create a local variable named total that is set to the calc_total() function. In this case, you must pass mealprice, tip, and tax to the function, so they must be placed between the parentheses. This should look like the following:

```
total = calc_total(mealprice, tip, tax)
```

Step 12: Add the following lines of code inside of calc_total(mealprice, tip, tax) function. The entire function should look like the following:

```
def calc_total(mealprice, tip, tax):
        total = mealprice + tip + tax
        return total
```

The first line is the function definition. It accepts mealprice, tip, and tax as parameters. The second line is to calculate the total of all three values added together. The third line returns the calculated total to the place where it is called.

Step 13: Inside of main() under the total = calc_total(mealprice, tip, tax) statement, call the print_info () function. In this case, you must pass mealprice, tip, tax, and total to the function, so they must be placed between the parentheses. This should look like the following:

```
print_info(mealprice, tip, tax, total)
```

Step 14: Add the following lines of code inside of print_info(mealprice, tip, tax, total) function. The entire function should look like the following:

```
def print_info(mealprice, tip, tax, total):
        print 'The meal price is $', mealprice
        print 'The tip is $', tip
        print 'The tax is $', tax
        print 'The total is $', total
```

The first line is the function definition. It accepts mealprice, tip, tax, and total as parameters. The following lines print the mealprice, the calculated tip, the calculated tax, and the calculated total.

Step 15: Run your module and fix any errors you may have. The most common errors may be that you have misspelled something when typing, or that your indentations are not aligned properly. When running your program, enter 24.50 as the meal price. Your output should look as follows:

```
Welcome to the tip and tax calculator program

Enter the meal price $24.50
The meal price is $ 24.5
The tip is $ 4.9
The tax is $ 1.47
The total is $ 30.87
```

Step 16: When your program is completed and you have tested your output in Step 15, copy and paste your work into a Word document. Save and print your document, then turn it in for grading.

Name: _____

Lab 2.7 – Programming Challenge 1: Retail Tax

This lab requires you to translate your work in the pseudocode and flowchart from Lab 2.2 and Lab 2.3 to actual code using Python. Read the following problem prior to completing the lab.

```
A retail company must file a monthly sales tax report
listing the total sales for the month, and the amount of
state and county sales tax collected. The state sales
tax rate is 4 percent and the county sales tax rate is 2
percent.

Write a program that asks the user to enter the total
sales for the month. The application should calculate
and display the following:
   •  The amount of county sales tax
   •  The amount of state sales tax
   •  The total sales tax (county plus state)
```

Consider the following functions for your program:
- main that calls your other functions
- inputData that will ask for the monthly sales
- calcCounty that will calculate the county tax
- calcState that will calculate the state tax
- calcTotal that will calculate the total tax
- printData that will display the county tax, the state tax, and the total tax

If your program is correct, sample output might look as follows:

```
Welcome to the total tax calculator program.

Enter the total sales for the month $12567
The county tax is $ 251.34
The state tax is $ 502.68
The total tax is $ 754.02
```

When your Python code is complete and correct, copy and paste your work into a Word document. Save and print your document, then turn it in for grading.

Lab 3: Decisions and Boolean Logic I
This lab accompanies Chapter 4 of *Starting Out with Programming Logic & Design*.

Name: _____

Lab 3.1 – Evaluating Conditions

Critical Review

A **relational operator** determines whether a specific relationship exists between two values.

Relational operators

Operator	Meaning	Boolean Expression
>	Greater than	X > Y
<	Less than	X < Y
>=	Greater than or equal to	X >= Y
<=	Less than or equal to	X <= Y
==	Equal to	X == Y
!=	Not equal to	X != Y

This lab requires you to think about possible true and false conditions using if statements.

Step 1: Consider the following values set to variables.
- myAge = 32
- yourAge = 18
- myNumber = 81
- yourNumber = 17
- votingAge = 18
- myName = "Katie"
- yourName = "Bob"

Step 2: Based on the values to the variables in Step 1, do the following conditions result in a true or false statement? (Reference Boolean Expressions, p. 119.)

The condition	True or False
myAge >= yourAge	
yourAge > myAge	
myAge == 45	
yourAge == votingAge	

votingAge <= yourAge	
myAge <= votingAge	
myName != yourName	
myNumber <= myAge	
yourNumber >= myAge	
yourNumber != 17	

Step 3: Based on the values to the variables in Step 1, what is the expected output? Hint: The output will be either what is printed to the screen, or nothing. (Reference Boolean Expressions, page 119.)

The condition	Expected Output

If myName == yourName Then
    print "We have the same name"
End If	

If myAge >= yourAge Then
    print "I am older or equal to your
    age"
End If	

If myName != "Katie" Then
    print "That is not my name"
End If	

If myName == "Katie" Then
    print "That is my name"
End If	

If myNumber == 17 Then
    print "My number is 17"
End If	

If myNumber >=80 Then
    print "My number is 80 or more"
End If	

If yourNumber <= yourAge Then
    print "Your number is less than or
    equal to your age"
End If	

If myNumber < yourNumber Then
    print "My number is less"
End If	

If yourAge >= votingAge Then
    print "You can vote"
End If	

If myAge < yourAge Then
    print "I am younger"
End If	

Name: _____

Lab 3.2 – Pseudocode and Decisions

Critical Review

Questions are often asked using an **if statement**, such as if(X > Y), whereas the question asked is, "is X greater than Y?"

The general structure of an if statement is
```
If condition Then
      Statement
      Statement
      Etc.
End If
```

This lab requires you to think about the steps that takes place in a program by writing pseudocode. Read the following problem prior to completing the lab.

> A retail company assigns a $5000 store bonus if monthly sales are $100,000 or more. Additionally, if their sales exceed 125% or more of their monthly goal of $90,000, then all employees will receive a message stating that they will get a day off.

Step 1: This program is most easily solved using just one variable. Declare the variables that you will need in the program, using the proper data type and documenting the purpose. Depending on your programming style, you may find additional variables are useful. If that is the case, adjust your program as necessary.

Variable Name	Purpose
	Stores the monthly sales

Step 2: Given the major task involved in this program, what modules might you consider including? List them, and also describe the purpose of the module.

Module Name	Purpose
Module getSales ()	Allows the user to enter the monthly sales.
salesBonus	This module will determine if a bonus should be awarded.
salesPercent	This module will determine if a day off should be awarded.

Step 3: Complete the pseudocode by writing the missing lines. Also, when writing your modules and making calls, be sure to pass necessary variables as arguments and accept them as reference parameters if they need to be modified in the module. (Reference Writing a Decision Structure in Pseudocode, p. 118.)

```
Module main ()
      //Declare local variables
      Declare Real monthlySales

      //Function calls
      Call getSales(monthlySales)

      _____

      _____


End Module

//this module takes in the required user input
Module getSales(Real Ref monthlySales)
      Display "Enter the total sales for the month."
      Input monthlySales
End Module

//this module will determine if a bonus is awarded
Module _____

      If monthlySales >=100000 Then
            Print "You get a bonus of $5,000!!!"
      End If
End Module

//this module will determine if all employees get a day
//off.  If sales are greater than or equal to 112500,
//then they get a day off.
Module _____
      If monthlySales >=112500 Then
            Print "YOU'VE BEEN AWARDED A DAY OFF."
      END IF

      _____

End Module
```

Name: _____

Lab 3.3 – Flowcharts

Critical Review

The flowchart symbol used to indicate some condition is a diamond. An `if` statement is called a single alternative decision structure. The code will only process if the decision is true.

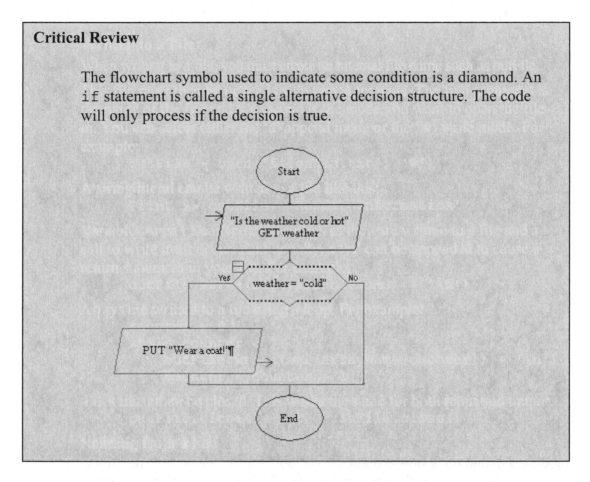

This lab requires you to convert your pseudocode in Lab 3.2 to a flowchart. Use an application such as Raptor or Visio. The following instructions assume you are using Raptor.

Step 1: Start Raptor and save your document as *Lab 3-3*. The *.rap* file extension will be added automatically. Start by adding a Comment box that declares your variables. Here is how your Comment box should look:

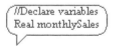

Step 2: The next step in your flowchart should be to call your methods. Below is a start of how your main should look:

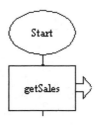

Step 3: Continue this process to add the additional methods you defined in Lab 3.2, Step 3.

Step 4: Click on the getSales tab and add the necessary code to enter the monthly sales. Your getSales method might look like the following:

Step 5: Click on the second module, which determines if a bonus of $5000 is awarded. Click the Selection symbol and add it between the start and the end of the module. Double-click on the diamond symbol and add the code to determine if monthlySales is greater than or equal to 100000. The enter selection condition should be written as follows:

Enter Selection Condition

Help

Enter selection condition.

Examples:
    Count = X+2
    Count != 5
    Score_Array[4] < 10
    Middle <= Y and Y <= Top

monthlySales >=100000

Done

Step 6: Drag an output symbol and drop it on the True line. Double-click on the output box and add text that prints, "You earned a $5000 bonus!" Your module should like this:

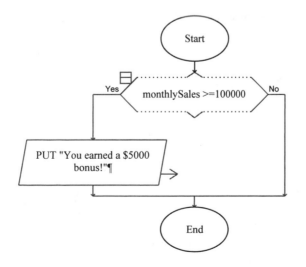

Step 7: Repeat the process in Step 6 to code your next module.

Step 8: When your program is complete, test the following monthly sales and ensure that the output matches the following. If your output is different, then review your decision statements.

Monthly Sales	Expected Output
monthlySales = 102500	You earned a $5000 bonus!
monthlySales = 90000	<nothing>
monthlySales= 112500	You earned a $5000 bonus! All employees get one day off!!!

Step 9: The final step is to print your finished flowchart. Inside Raptor, select File and the Print to Clipboard from the menu. Inside Word, select Edit and Paste. You will have to do this for each module you created. Save and print your document. Turn it in for grading.

Name: _____

Lab 3.4 – Python Code

Critical Review

In Python, we use the **if statement** to write a single alternative decision structure. Here is the general format of the `if` statement:

```
if condition:
    statement
    statement
    etc.
```

For simplicity, we will refer to the first line as the if clause. The if clause begins with the word if, followed by a condition, which is an expression that will be evaluated as either true or false. A colon appears after the condition. Beginning at the next line is a block of statements.

When the `if` statement executes, the condition is tested. If the condition is true, the statements that appear in the block following the if clause are executed. If the condition is false, the statements in the block are skipped.

When strings are evaluated in a condition, single quotation marks are used. For example:

```
name1 = 'Mary'
name2 = 'Mark'

if name1 != name2:
        print 'The names are not the same.'

if name1 == 'Mary'
        print 'The name is Mary.'
```

Step 1: Start the IDLE Environment for Python. Prior to entering code, save your file by clicking on File and then Save. Select your location and save this file as *Lab3-4.py*. Be sure to include the .py extension.

Step 2: Document the first few lines of your program to include your name, the date, and a brief description of what the program does. Use this description of the program:

```
#This program will demonstrate how to use decision
#statements in Python.
```

Step 3: Start your program with the following code:

```
#This program determines if a bonus should be
awarded

#The main function
def main():
    print 'Welcome to the program'
    monthlySales = getSales()  # gets sales


#This function gets the monthly sales
def getSales():
    monthlySales = input('Enter the monthly sales
$')
    monthlySales = float(monthlySales)
    return monthlySales

#calls main
main()
```

Step 4: Add a function call to the method that determines if a bonus is awarded. The call should be in main and process after `monthlySales = getSales(.)` Be sure to pass monthlySales to the function as an argument since that will be needed to determine if a bonus is awarded. Your code might look as follows:

```
#Function call to determine bonus
isBonus(monthlySales)
```

Step 5: Under the getSales() function, code the function that will determine if a bonus is awarded. Be sure to accept monthlySales in the parameter list. Also, note that the if statement is followed by a colon, and the print statement inside must be tabbed over.

```
def isBonus(monthlySales):
    if monthlySales >= 100000:
        print "You have earned a $5,000 bonus!!!"
```

Step 6: Repeat the process in Step 4 to make a function call to the method that determines if all employees get a day off.

Step 7: Repeat the process in Step 5 to code the function that will determine if all employees should get a day off.

Step 8: Click Run and Run Module to see how your program processes. Test the following monthlySales values to verify the expected output.

Monthly Sales	Expected Output
monthlySales = 102500	You earned a $5000 bonus!
monthlySales = 90000	<nothing>
monthlySales= 112500	You earned a $5000 bonus! All employees get one day off!!!

When your Python code is complete and correct, copy and paste your work into a Word document. Save and print your document, then turn it in for grading.

Name: _____

Lab 3.5 – Programming Challenge 1: Guess the Secrets

For the following programming problem, write:
1. the algorithm
2. the pseudocode
3. the flowchart
4. Python code

Copy and paste your work into a Word document, labeling each section. Save and print your document, then turn it in for grading.

Guess the Secrets

> Write a program that will ask the user to enter a person's age, weight, and birth month. Your program will compare the entered values to the following and print the appropriate responses. Be sure to use modules.

The Secret Answers	The Comparison	The Printed Response
age = 25	If the guessed age is less than or equal to 25	Congratulations, the age is 25 or less.
weight = 128	If the guessed weight is greater than or equal to 128	Congratulations, the weight is 128 or more.
birthMonth = 'April'	If the guessed birth month is equal to April	Congratulations, the birth month is April.

> Hints: This program can be written a few different ways. It is suggested that only three variables are used to store the guessed answers to age, weight, and birthMonth. The pseudocode for main might look as follows:

```
Module main ()
      //Declare local variables
      Declare Integer age
      Declare Integer weight
      Declare String birthMonth

      //Function calls
      Call getAge(age)
      Call getWeight(weight)
      Call getMonth(birthMonth)
      Call correctAnswers(age, weight, birthMonth)
End Module
```

If the program is written properly, sample output should look as follows:

Sample 1:
      //Input
      Enter your guess for age: 20
      Enter your guess for weight: 140
      Enter your guess for birth month: March

      //Output
      Congratulations, the age is 25 or less.
      Congratulations, the weight is 128 or more.

Sample 2:
      //Input
      Enter your guess for age: 32
      Enter your guess for weight: 119
      Enter your guess for birth month: April

      //Output
      Congratulations, the birth month is April.

Sample 3:
      //Input
      Enter your guess for age: 58
      Enter your guess for weight: 128
      Enter your guess for birth month: January

      //Output
      Congratulations, the weight is 128 or more.

Lab 4: Decisions and Boolean Logic II

This lab accompanies Chapter 4 of *Starting Out with Programming Logic & Design*.

Name: _____

Lab 4.1 – Logical Operators and Dual Alternative Decisions

Critical Review

The logical **AND** operator and the logical **OR** operator allow you to connect multiple Boolean expressions to create a compound expression.

The logical **NOT** operator reverses the truth of a Boolean expression.

When using the AND operator, both conditions must be true in order for the statements within an `if` statement to process.

When using the OR operator, either condition must be true in order for the statements within an `if` statement to process.

A dual alternative decision structure will execute one group of statements if its Boolean expression is true, or another group if its Boolean expression is false.

The general structure of an if-then-else statement is

```
If condition Then
        Statement
        Statement
        Etc.
Else
        Statement
        Statement
        Etc.
End If
```

This lab requires you to think about possible true and false conditions using `if` statements.

Step 1: Consider the following values set to variables.
- myAge = 32
- yourAge = 18
- myNumber = 81
- yourNumber = 17
- votingAge = 18

Step 2: Based on the values to the variables in Step 1, what is the expected output? Hint: The output will either be what is printed to the screen, or nothing. (Reference Logical Operators, p. 146.)

Condition	Expected Output

If myAge == 31 AND yourAge < myAge Then
   Display "My age is 31 and your age is less than that"
End If	

If myAge <= 35 AND myAge >= 32 Then
   Display "My age is between 32 and 35"
End If	

If yourAge == votingAge OR yourAge > votingAge Then
   Display "You can vote"
End If	

If myNumber == 83 OR yourNumber == 83 Then
   Display "One of our numbers is 83"
End If	

Step 3: Based on the values to the variables in Step 1, what is the expected output? (Reference Dual Alternative Decision Structures, p. 125.)

Condition	Expected Output

If myAge == 31 AND yourAge < myAge Then
   Display "My age is 31 and your age is less than that"
Else
   Display "Our ages do not qualify"
End If	

If myAge <= 35 AND myAge >= 32 Then
   Display "My age is between 32 and 35"
Else
   Display "My age is not within that range"
End If	

If yourAge == votingAge OR yourAge > votingAge Then
   Display "You can vote"
Else
   Display "You cannot vote"
End If	

If myNumber == 83 OR yourNumber == 83 Then
   Display "One of our numbers is 83"
Else
   Display "83 is not our numbers"
End If	

Name: _____

Lab 4.2 – Pseudocode: Dual Alternative Decisions

Critical Review

> A **dual alternative decision structure** will execute one group of statements if its Boolean expression is true, or another group if its Boolean expression is false.
>
> The general structure of an if-then-else statement is
> ```
> If condition Then
>         Statement
>         Statement
>         Etc.
> Else
>         Statement
>         Statement
>         Etc.
> End If
> ```

Module Review

> Recall the difference between a reference variable and a value variable. Reference variables are used in the following lab when the value of the variable is modified in the module. You'll notice some parameter lists include the keyword Ref before the variable that is going to change within the module.

This lab requires you to think about the steps that takes place in a program by writing pseudocode.

Recall the retail company program from Lab 3.2. The company now wants to modify their bonus program to include different levels and types and eliminate the day-off program. The new program is as follows:

```
A retail company assigns a $5000 store bonus if monthly
sales are more than $100,000 otherwise a $500 store
bonus is awarded. Additionally, they are doing away with
the previous day off program and now using a percent of
sales increase to determine if employees get individual
bonuses. If sales increased by at least 4% then all
employees get a $50 bonus. If they do not, then
individual bonuses are 0.
```

Step 1: To accommodate the changes to the program, create the additional variables needed.

- Create a variable named storeAmount to hold the store bonus amount.
- Create a variable named empAmount to hold the individual bonus amount.
- Create a variable named salesIncrease to hold the percent of increase.

```
//Declare local variables
Declare Real monthlySales
```

_____

_____

_____

Step 2: The first module in program is getSales(). Since this is still required, leave this module as is. This module should be written as follows:

```
//MODULE 1
//this module takes in the required user input
Module getSales(Real Ref monthlySales)
     Display "Enter the total sales for the month."
     Input monthlySales
End Module
```

Step 3: The second module in the program was isBonus(). Since there are two types of bonuses now, rename this module and the module call to storeBonus(). Write an if-then-else statement within this module that will set the bonus amount to either 5000 or 500. Also, pass the variable storeAmount to the module as a reference. Complete the missing lines. (Reference Dual Alternative Decision Structures, p. 125.)

```
//MODULE 2
//this module will determine what the bonus levels are
Module _____(Real monthlySales, Real Ref _____)
     If monthlySales >=100000 Then

          Set _____ = 5000

     _____

          Set _____ = 500
     End If
End Module
```

Step 4: Write a module that will ask the user to enter the percent of sales increase in decimal format. This module will have to accept salesIncrease as a reference. Complete the missing lines.

```
//MODULE 3
//this module takes in percent of increase in decimal
//format such as .02 for 2 percent.
Module getIncrease(Real Ref _____)
     Display "_____."
     Input _____
End Module
```

Step 5: Write a module that will determine individual bonuses. If the sales increase percent was 4% or more, then all employees get a $50 bonus. If the 4% increase was not reached, then bonus amount should be set to zero. This module should be called empBonus and accept salesIncrease as a normal variable and empAmount as a reference.

```
//MODULE 4
//this module will determine what the bonus levels are
Module _____(Real _____, Real Ref _____)
     If salesIncrease >=_____ Then
          Set _____ = 50
     Else
          Set _____ = 0
     End If
End Module
```

Step 6: Write a module that will print the store bonus and the employee bonus amount. Name this module printBonus() and pass the two necessary variables.

```
//MODULE 5
//this module will display store and employee bonus info.
Module _____(Real _____, Real _____)
     Display "The store bonus is $", _____
     Display "The employee bonus is $", _____
End Module
```

Step 7: The final step in completing the pseudocode is to call all the modules with the proper arguments. Complete the missing lines.

```
Module main ()
        //Declare local variables
        Declare Real monthlySales
        Declare Real storeAmount
        Declare Real empAmount
        Declare Real salesIncrease

        //Function calls
        Call getSales(monthlySales)
        Call getIncrease(salesIncrease)

        Call _____(_____, _____)

        Call _____(_____, _____)

        Call _____(_____, _____)

End Module
```

Name: _____

Lab 4.3 – Pseudocode: Nested Decision Structures

Critical Review

To test more than one condition, a decision structure can be nested inside another decision structure. This structure can become very complex, and often an **if-then-else-if** statement is used instead.

The general structure of the if-then-else-if statement is

```
If condition_1 Then
      Statement
      Statement
      Etc.
Else If condition_2 Then
      Statement
      Statement
      Etc.
Insert as many Else If clauses as necessary
Else
      Statement
      Statement
      Etc.
End If
```

A case structure lets the value of a variable or an expression determine which path of execution the program will take. This is often used as an alternative to a nested if-else decision.

The company now wants to add additional levels to their store and employee bonuses. The new levels are as follows:

```
Store bonuses:
If store sales are $80,000 or more, store bonus is $3000
If store sales are $90,000 or more, store bonus is $4000
If store sales are $100,000 or more, store bonus is
$5000
If store sales are $110,000 or more, store bonus is
$6000

Employee bonuses:
If percent of increase is 3% or more, employee bonus is
$40
```

```
If percent of increase is 4% or more, employee bonus is
$50
If percent of increase is 5% or more, employee bonus is
$75

*Note: Bonuses are not cumulative. For example, if sales
are $95,000, only a bonus of $4000 is awarded, not $3000
and $4000.
```

Step 1: Modify the storeBonus module to write a nested if-else statement to set the new bonus levels. Complete the missing lines.
(Reference The if-then-else Statement, p. 140.)

```
//MODULE 2
//this module will determine what the bonus levels are
Module storeBonus (Real monthlySales, Real Ref
storeAmount)
      If monthlySales >= 110000 Then
            Set storeAmount = 6000

      Else If monthlySales >= _____ Then

            Set storeAmount = _____
      Else if monthlySales >= _____ Then

            Set storeAmount = _____
      Else if monthlySales >= _____ Then

            Set storeAmount = _____
      Else
            Set storeAmount = 0
      End If
End Module
```

Step 2: Modify the empBonus module to write a nested if-else statement to set the new bonus levels. Complete the missing lines.
(Reference The if-then-else Statement, p. 140.)

```
//MODULE 4
//this module will determine what the bonus levels are
Module empBonus (Real salesIncrease, Real Ref empAmount)
      If salesIncrease >= .05 Then
            Set empAmount = 75

      Else If salesIncrease >= _____ Then

            Set empAmount = _____
      Else if salesIncrease >= _____ Then

            Set empAmount = _____
```

```
        Else
             Set empAmount = 0
        End If
End Module
```

Step 3: Modify Module 5 by adding an `if` statement that will print a message if both the store bonus and the employee bonus are the highest amounts possible. (Reference Logical Operators, p. 147.)

```
//MODULE 5
//this module will display store and employee bonus info.
Module printBonus(Real storeAmount, Real empAmount)
        Display "The store bonus is $", storeAmount
        Display "The employee bonus is $", empAmount

        If storeAmount == _____ AND empAmount == _____ Then
             Display "Congrats! You have reached the
             highest bonus amounts possible!"
        End If
End Module
```

Name: _____

Lab 4.4 – Flowcharts

Critical Review

A dual alternative decision structure has two possible paths of execution – one path is taken if a condition is true, and the other path is taken if the condition is false.

A diamond with a true and false value is used in flowcharting a dual alternative decision structure.

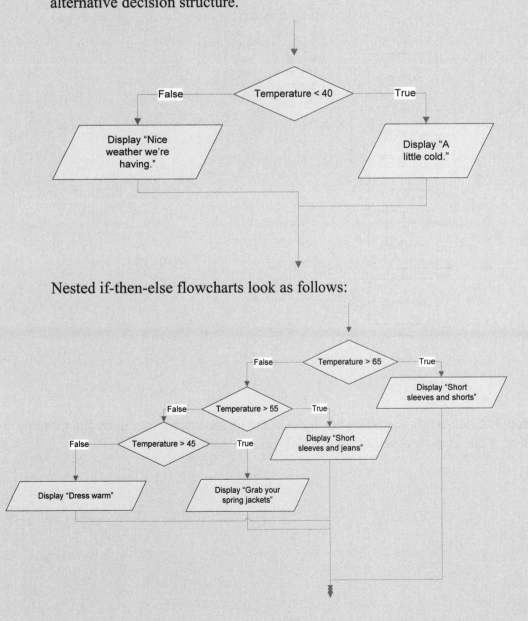

Nested if-then-else flowcharts look as follows:

This lab requires you to convert your pseudocode in Lab 4.3 to a flowchart. Use an application such as Raptor or Visio. These instructions assume you are using Raptor.

Step 1: Start Raptor and save your document as *Lab 4-4*. The *.rap* file extension will be added automatically. Start by adding a Comment box that declares your variables.

Step 2: The next step in your flowchart should be to call your methods. Main should look as follows. Be sure to click yes to add new tabs for each module.

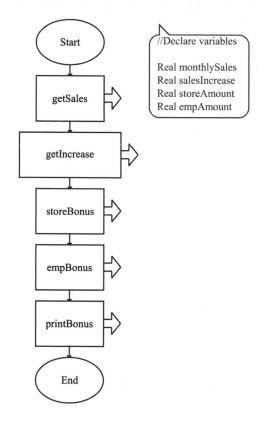

Step 3: Click on the getSales tab and add the necessary code to enter the monthly sales. Your getSales method might look like the following:

Step 4: Click on the getIncrease tab and add the necessary code to enter the percent of increase in sales. Since percentages can be entered different ways, you should specify to the user how to enter the number. Either method is fine. One method follows:

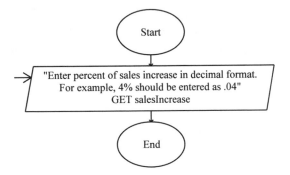

Here is a different method whereby the number entered is divided by 100:

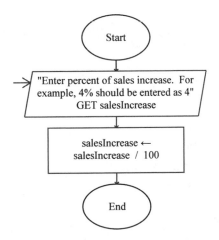

Step 5: Click on the storeBonus tab and add the nested if-then-else statement from Lab 4.3, Step 1. Do not forget the final else, setting storeAmount to 0. The start of your module should look as follows, and you should have a total of four decisions:

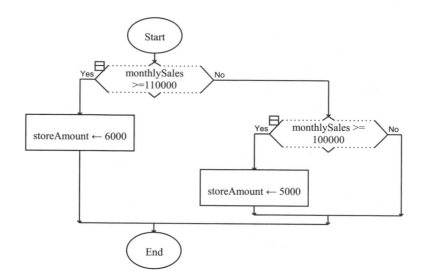

Step 6: Click on the empBonus tab and add the nested if-then-else statement from Lab 4.3, Step 2. Do not forget the final else, setting empAmount to 0. The start of your module should look as follows, and you should have a total of three decisions:

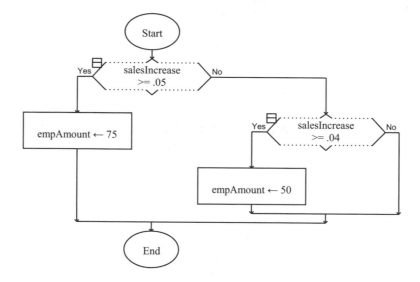

Step 7: Click the printBonus tab and add the necessary code from Lab 4.3, Step 3. The module should look as follows:

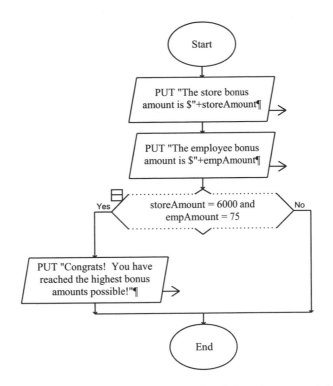

Step 8: When your program is complete, test the following monthly sales and sales increases to ensure that the output matches the following. If your output is different, then review your code.

Input Values	Expected Output
monthlySales = 120500 salesIncrease = 5	The store bonus amount is $6000 The employee bonus amount is $75 Congrats! You have reached the highest bonus amounts possible!
monthlySales = 93400 salesIncrease = 5	The store bonus amount is $4000 The employee bonus amount is $75
monthlySales = 75000 salesIncrease = 1.5	The store bonus amount is $0 The employee bonus amount is $0
monthlySales = 82000 salesIncrease = 3.6	The store bonus amount is $3000 The employee bonus amount is $40
monthlySales = 125000 salesIncrease = 4.5	The store bonus amount is $6000 The employee bonus amount is $50

Step 9: The final step is to print out your finished flowchart and turn it in to your instructor. Inside Raptor, select File and the Print to Clipboard from the menu. Open Word, then select Edit and Paste to put your flowchart in a Word document. Save and print. You will have to do this for each module you created.

Name: _____

Lab 4.5 – Python Code

Critical Review

In code we write a dual alternative decision structure as an `if-else` statement. Here is the general format of the `if-else` statement:

```
if condition:
    statement
    statement
    etc.
else:
    statement
    statement
    etc.
```

Here is the general format of the `if-elif-else` statement:

```
if condition_1:
    statement
    statement
    etc.
elif condition_2:
    statement
    statement
    etc.
```

Insert as many elif clauses as necessary...

```
else:
    statement
    statement
    etc.
```

The logical operators `and`, `or`, and `not` are used in Python to connect Boolean expressions.

Step 1: Start the IDLE Environment for Python. Prior to entering code, save your file by clicking on File and then Save. Select your location and save this file as *Lab4-5.py*. Be sure to include the .py extension.

Step 2: Document the first few lines of your program to include your name, the date, and a brief description of what the program does.

Step 3: Start your program with the following code:

```
#Lab 4-5
#The main function
def main():
    monthlySales = getSales() #call to get sales


#This function gets the monthly sales
def getSales():
    monthlySales = input('Enter the monthly sales $')
    monthlySales = float(monthlySales)
    return monthlySales

#This function gets the percent of increase in sales
def getIncrease():

#This function determines the storeAmount bonus
def storeBonus():

#This function determines the empAmount bonus
def empBonus():

#This function prints the bonus information
def printBonus():

#calls main
main()
```

Step 4: Under the getIncrease function, add the necessary code to allow the user to input the sales increase. Your code might look as follows:

```
#This function gets the percent of increase in sales
def getIncrease():
    salesIncrease = input('Enter percent of sales
    increase. For example 4% should be entered as 4: ')
    salesIncrease = float(salesIncrease)
    salesIncrease = salesIncrease / 100
    return salesIncrease
```

Step 5: Under the call to getSales(), add a function call to getIncrease().

```
salesIncrease = getIncrease() #call to get sales increase
```

Step 6: Under the storeBonus function, add the necessary code so that the program will determine what the proper storeAmount variable should have. This function might look as follows:

```
#This function determines the storeAmount bonus
def storeBonus(monthlySales):
    if monthlySales >=110000:
        storeAmount = 6000
    elif monthlySales >=100000:
        storeAmount = 5000
    elif monthlySales >=90000:
        storeAmount = 4000
    elif monthlySales >=80000:
        storeAmount = 3000
    else:
        storeAmount = 0
    return storeAmount
```

Step 7: Under the call to getIncrease(), add a function call to storeBonus().

```
#call to get the store bonus
storeAmount = storeBonus(monthlySales)
```

Step 8: Repeat a process similar to steps 6 and 7 for writing the empBonus() function and making a call to it. Recall, this function uses salesIncrease to determine empAmount.

Step 9: Code the printBonus() function to print the storeAmount and empAmount. This function might look as follows:

```
#This function prints the bonus information
def printBonus(storeAmount, empAmount):
    print 'The store bonus amount is $', storeAmount
    print 'The employee bonus amount is $', empAmount
    if storeAmount == 6000 and empAmount == 75:
        print 'Congrats! You have reached the highest
bonus amounts possible!'
```

Step 10: Under the call to empBonus(), add a function call to printBonus. This call might look as follows:

```
printBonus(storeAmount, empAmount) #call to print amounts
```

Step 11: Click Run and Run Module to see how your program processes. Test the following values to verify the expected output.

Input Values	Expected Output
monthlySales = 120500 salesIncrease = 5	The store bonus amount is $ 6000 The employee bonus amount is $ 75 Congrats! You have reached the highest bonus amounts possible!
monthlySales = 93400 salesIncrease = 5	The store bonus amount is $4000 The employee bonus amount is $75
monthlySales = 75000 salesIncrease = 1.5	The store bonus amount is $0 The employee bonus amount is $0
monthlySales = 82000 salesIncrease = 3.6	The store bonus amount is $3000 The employee bonus amount is $40
monthlySales = 125000 salesIncrease = 4.5	The store bonus amount is $6000 The employee bonus amount is $50

Step 12: Execute your program so that it works. When your Python code is complete and correct, copy and paste your work into a Word document. Save and print your document, then turn it in for grading.

Name: _____

Lab 4.6 – Programming Challenge 1: Tip, Tax, and Total

For the following programming problem, write:
1. the algorithm
2. the pseudocode
3. the flowchart
4. Python code

Copy and paste your work into a Word document, labeling each section. Save and print your document, then turn it in for grading.

Tip, Tax and Total

Recall the Tip, Tax, and Total program from Lab 2.6. Modify your program to include new requirements.

> Write a program that will calculate a XXX% tip and a 6% tax on a meal price. The user will enter the meal price and the program will calculate tip, tax, and the total. The total is the meal price plus the tip plus the tax. Your program will then display the values of tip, tax, and total.
>
> The restaurant now wants to change the program so that the tip percent is based on the meal price. The new amounts are as follows:

Meal Price Range	Tip Percent
.01 to 5.99	10%
6 to 12.00	13%
12.01 to 17.00	16%
17.01 to 25.00	19%
25.01 and more	22%

Lab 5: Repetition Structures I
This lab accompanies Chapter 5 of *Starting Out with Programming Logic & Design*.

Name: _____

Lab 5.1 – Repetition Structures Pseudocode: Condition-Controlled Loops

Critical Review

A **repetition structure** causes a statement or set of statements to execute repeatedly.
Repetition structures are used to perform the same task over and over.

Repetition structures are commonly called loops.

A **condition-controlled loop** uses a true/false condition to control the number of times that it repeats.

The general structure of a **While loop** with a condition-controlled statement is:

```
//Declare loop control variable
While condition
     statement
     statement
     etc.
     //Ask Question that changes the loop control
     //variable
End While
```

The general structure of a **Do While loop** with a condition-controlled statement is:

```
//Declare loop control variable
Do
     statement
     statement
     etc.
     //Ask Question that changes the loop control
     //variable
While Condition
```

This lab requires you to implement a condition-controlled loop.

Step 1: Examine the following main Module from Lab 4.2. Loops are commonly used to call modules multiple times. The best design is to use a loop around the module calls in Main.

```
Module main ()
      //Declare local variables
      Declare Real monthlySales
      Declare Real storeAmount
      Declare Real empAmount
      Declare Real salesIncrease

      //Function calls
      Call getSales(monthlySales)
      Call getIncrease(salesIncrease)
      Call storeBonus(monthlySales, storeAmount)
      Call empBonus(salesIncrease, empAmount)
      Call printBonus(storeAmount, empAmount)
End Module
```

Step 2: In the space provided, create a loop control variable named keepGoing of the data type string. Initialize this variable to "y."
(Reference Modularizing the Code in the Body of a Loop, p. 172.)

Step 3: In the space provided, write a while statement.

```
Module main ()
      //Declare local variables
      Declare Real monthlySales
      Declare Real storeAmount
      Declare Real empAmount
      Declare Real salesIncrease


      _____

      //Function calls

      While _____
            Call getSales(monthlySales)
            Call getIncrease(salesIncrease)
            Call storeBonus(monthlySales, storeAmount)
            Call empBonus(salesIncrease, empAmount)
            Call printBonus(storeAmount, empAmount)
            Display "Do you want to run the program
            again? (Enter y for yes.)"

            Input
            _____
      End While
End Module
```

Step 4: In the space provided, create a loop control variable named keepGoing of the data type string. Initialize this variable to "y."
(Reference Writing a Do-While Loop, p. 175.)

Step 5: In the space provided, write a do-while statement.

```
Module main ()
      //Declare local variables
      Declare Real monthlySales
      Declare Real storeAmount
      Declare Real empAmount
      Declare Real salesIncrease


      _____


      //Function calls
      Do
            Call getSales(monthlySales)
            Call getIncrease(salesIncrease)
            Call storeBonus(monthlySales, storeAmount)
            Call empBonus(salesIncrease, empAmount)
            Call printBonus(storeAmount, empAmount)
            Display "Do you want to run the program
            again? (Enter y for yes.)"

            Input _____

      While _____
End Module
```

Name: _____

Lab 5.2 – Repetition Structures Pseudocode: Counter-Controlled Loops

Critical Review

A **counter-controlled loop** repeats a specific number of times.

The loop keeps a count of the number of times that it iterates, and when the count reaches a specified value, the loop stops.

A variable, known as a **counter variable**, is used to store the number of iterations that it has performed.

The three actions that take place are initialization, test, and increment.
- Initialization: Before the loop begins, the counter variable is initialized to a starting value.
- Test: The loop tests the counter variable by comparing it to a maximum value.
- Increment: To increment a variable means to increase its value. This is done by adding 1 to the loop control variable.

Any loop can be used with a counter-controlled loop.

A running total is a sum that accumulates with each iteration of a loop. The variable used to keep the running total is called an **accumulator**.

This lab requires you to write a complete program using a condition-controlled loop, a counter-controlled loop, and an accumulator. The problem is as follows:

```
Write a program that will allow a grocery store to keep
track of the total number of bottles collected for
recycling for seven days. The program should allow the
user to enter the number of bottles returned for each of
seven days. The program will calculate the total number
of bottles returned for the week and the amount paid out
(the total returned times 10 cents.) The output of the
program should include the total number of bottles
returned and the total paid out.
```

Step 1: In the pseudocode below, declare the following variables under the documentation for Step 1.
- A variable called totalBottles that is initialized to 0
  - This variable will store the accumulated bottle values
- A variable called counter and that is initialized to 1
  - This variable will control the loop
- A variable called todayBottles that is initialized to 0
  - This variable will store the number of bottles returned on a day
- A variable called totalPayout that is initialized to 0
  - This variable will store the calculated value of totalBottles times .10
- A variable called keepGoing that is initialized to "y"
  - This variable will be used to run the program again

Step 2: In the pseudocode below, make calls to the following functions under the documentation for Step 2.
- A function call to getBottles that passes totalBottles, todayBottles, and counter.
- A function called calcPayout that passes totalPayout and totalBottles.
- A function called printInfo that passes totalBottles and totalPayout

Step 3: In the pseudocode below, write a condition-controlled while loop around your function calls using the keepGoing variable under the documentation for Step 3.

Complete Steps 1-3 below:

```
Module main ()

        //Step 1: Declare variables below

        _____

        _____

        _____

        _____

        _____


        //Step 3: Loop to run program again

        While  _____

               //Step 2: Call functions

               _____

               _____

               _____
```

```
            Display "Do you want to run the program
            again? (Enter y for yes.)"
            Input _____
      End While          ,
   End Module
```

Step 4: In the pseudocode below, write the missing lines including:
   a. The missing parameter list
   b. The missing condition (Hint: should run seven iterations)
   c. The missing input variable
   d. The missing accumulator
   e. The increment statement for the counter

```
//getBottles module

Module
getBottles(a._____)

      While b._____

            Display "Enter number of bottles returned for
            the day:"

            Input c._____

            d. _____

            e. _____

      End While
   End Module
```

Step 5: In the pseudocode below, write the missing lines including:
   a. The missing parameter list
   b. The missing calculation

```
//getBottles module

Module
calcPayout(a._____)

      totalPayout = 0 //resets to 0 for multiple runs

      b. _____
   End Module
```

Step 6: In the pseudocode below, write the missing lines including:
   a. The missing parameter list
   b. The missing display statement

85

c. The missing display statement

```
//printInfo module
Module
printInfo(a._____)
        b.  _____
        c.  _____
End Module
```

Name: _____

Lab 5.3 – Flowcharts

Critical Review

In a **while loop**, the question is asked *first*. After the statements process, the control goes back above the condition.

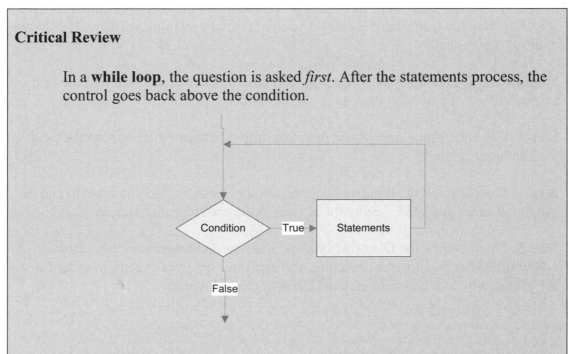

In a **do-while loop**, the question is asked *last*. The statements always process at least one time.

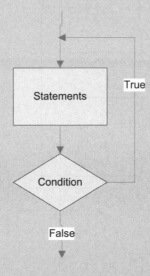

In Raptor, you can place the modules before or after the condition depending on whether you want to use a do-while or a while loop.

This lab requires you to convert your pseudocode in Lab 5.2 to a flowchart. Use an application such as Raptor or Visio. These instructions assume you are using Raptor.

Step 1: Start Raptor and save your document as *Lab 5-3*. The *.rap* file extension will be added automatically. Start by adding a Comment box that declares your variables. The only variable from Lab 5.2 that is different is the keepGoing variable. Name this endProgram instead.

Step 2: Click the Loop symbol and drag and drop it between the Start and the End symbol.

Step 3: Click the Input symbol and drag and drop it between the Loop symbol and the Diamond symbol.

Step 4: Double-click the Input symbol and ask the question "Do you want to end the program? Enter yes or no:" Store the answer in the endProgram variable.

Step 5: Double-click the Diamond symbol, and type endProgram = "yes" as the condition. When the program executes, the user must type yes exactly in order for the program to end. Now, main should look as the following:

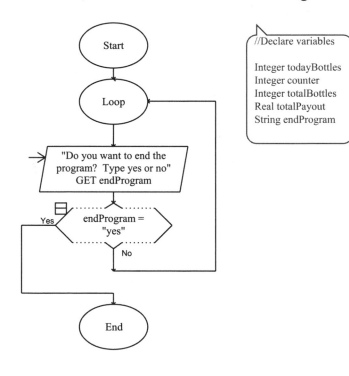

Step 6: The next step in your flowchart should be to call your methods. Add your modules under the Loop oval. Be sure to click yes to add new tabs for each module. Now, main should look like this:

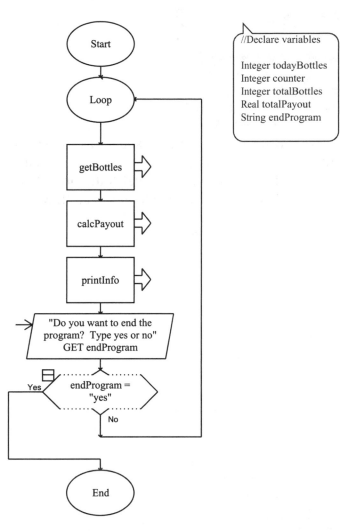

Step 7: Click on the getBottles tab. Add a Loop symbol between the Start and End symbols. Double-click the Diamond symbol and enter the condition as counter >7.

Step 8: Add an Input symbol and add the code, "Enter the number of bottles returned for today:" Store the value in the todayBottles variable.

Step 9: Add an Assignment symbol next and set totalBottles to totalBottles + todayBottles.

Step 10: Add another Assignment symbol next and set counter to counter + 1.

Step 11: Save your program and try running it. You'll notice an error occur when the loop starts processing in the getBottles module. This is because totalBottles does not have a starting value.

Step 12: To fix the error, to set the counter to 1, and to reset the todayBottles back to 0 for multiple repetitions, add three Assignment symbols above the Loop symbol. In one symbol, set counter to 1. In the second, set totalBottles to 0. In the third, set todayBottles to 0. Your getBottles module should look as follows:

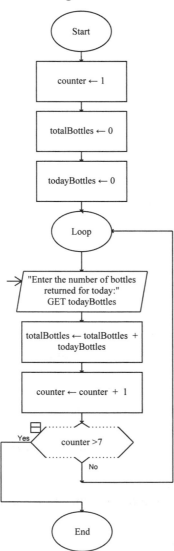

Step 13: Click the calcPayout module and add an Assignment symbol. Set totalPayout to totalBottles times .10.

Step 14: Click the printInfo module and add two Output symbols that print the total bottles returned and the total amount paid out.

Step 15: Test your program against the following values. If there is an error, go back through the steps to locate the problem.

Input Values	Expected Output
Seven days of bottles: 346 238 638 890 1035 899 536	The total number of bottles collected was: 4582 The total amount paid out was $458.2000

Step 16: The final step is to print out your finished flowchart and turn it in to your instructor. Inside Raptor, select File and the Print to Clipboard from the menu. Open Word, then select Edit and Paste to put your flowchart in a Word document. Save and print.

Name: _____

Lab 5.4 – Python Code

Critical Review

In Python, you use the **while statement** to write a condition-controlled loop. The loop has two parts:
 (1) a condition that is tested for a true or false value, and
 (2) a statement or set of statements that is repeated as long as the condition is true.

A while loop can also be used for counter-controlled loops.

Here is the general format of the `while` loop in Python:

```
while condition:
    statement
    statement
    etc.
```

Since the while loop is a pre-test, it is important to initialize your loop control variable to a starting value so that the first iteration will be true.

As with all loops, be sure to change the loop control variable either by incrementing or asking a question.

The goal of this lab is to convert the Bottle Return program to Python code.

Step 1: Start the IDLE Environment for Python. Prior to entering code, save your file by clicking on File and then Save. Select your location and save this file as *Lab5-4.py*. Be sure to include the .py extension.

Step 2: Document the first few lines of your program to include your name, the date, and a brief description of what the program does.

Step 3: Start your program with the following code for main:

```
#Lab 5-4 The Bottle Return Program

#the main function
def main():

#calls main
main()
```

Step 4: Python only supports While loops, so endProgram must be initialized to 'no.' Under def main():, create a variable called endProgram and set it to 'no' such as:

```
endProgram = 'no'
```

Step 5: The next step is to write a while statement with the condition of endProgram == 'no':. The statement should be aligned with the statement in Step 4. The code should be as follows:

```
while endProgram == 'no':
```

Step 6: The code inside of the while statement should be tabbed over and include your function calls. The function getBottles() will return totalBottles so the call should be set to that variable. The function calcPayout should pass totalBottles as an argument and will return totalPayout from the function. The function printInfo should pass totalBottles and totalPayout as arguments. The code should look like this:

```
totalBottles = getBottles()
totalPayout = calcPayout(totalBottles)
printInfo(totalBottles, totalPayout)
```

Step 7: The next step is to modify the loop control variable. This is done with a simple raw_input statement, such as:

```
endProgram = raw_input('Do you want to end the program?
(Enter yes or no): ')
```

Step 8: The next function to code is getBottles. Write a definition for getBottles that accepts no arguments. The code should look as follows:

```
#this function will get the number of bottles returned
def getBottles():
```

Step 9: The first step in your function should be to set your variables to values. In Python and most programming languages, variables need to have a starting value before they can be used. This also allows for a reset of the variables when the program runs again. Set totalBottles and todayBottles to 0 and counter to 1. Your code should look as follows:

```
totalBottles = 0
todayBottles = 0
counter = 1
```

Step 10: Write a while loop with the condition of counter <= 7. This code should look like this:

```
while counter <= 7:
```

Step 11: Inside the while loop, write a statement that allows the user to enter the number of bottles for today. This code should look as follows:

```
todayBottles = input('Enter number of bottles for today: ')
```

Step 12: Next, write the accumulator statement. This code should look as follows:

```
totalBottles = totalBottles + todayBottles
```

Step 13: The last statement inside the loop should increment counter by one so the loop will end after seven iterations. This code should look as follows:

```
counter = counter + 1
```

Step 14: The final statement in the getBottles function is to return totalBottles back to main. This code should look as follows:

```
return totalBottles
```

Step 15: Create a function definition for calcPayment that accepts totalBottles in the parameter list. This function should first reset totalPayout to 0. This is done so that on multiple iterations of the program, totalPayout is reset to 0. The second step in this function is to calculate totalPayout as totalBottles times .10. The last step is to return totalPayout. Your code should look as follows:

```
#this function will calculate the payout
def calcPayout(totalBottles):
    totalPayout = 0
    totalPayout = totalBottles * .10
    return totalPayout
```

Step 16: The final function is this program is printInfo. This function accepts two variables in the parameter list so that it can display the total number of bottles returned and the total amount paid out. Your code should look as follows:

```
#this function will display the information
def printInfo(totalBottles, totalPayout):
    print 'The total number of bottles collected was',
    totalBottles
    print 'The total paid out was $', totalPayout
```

Step 17: Click Run and Run Module to see how your program processes. Test the following values to verify the expected output.

```
>>>

Enter number of bottles for today: 346
Enter number of bottles for today: 238
Enter number of bottles for today: 638
Enter number of bottles for today: 890
Enter number of bottles for today: 1035
Enter number of bottles for today: 899
Enter number of bottles for today: 536
The total number of bottles collected was 4582
The total paid out was $ 458.2

Do you want to end the program? (Enter yes or no): no

Enter number of bottles for today: 425
Enter number of bottles for today: 342
Enter number of bottles for today: 235
Enter number of bottles for today: 539
Enter number of bottles for today: 485
Enter number of bottles for today: 321
Enter number of bottles for today: 128
The total number of bottles collected was 2475
The total paid out was $ 247.5

Do you want to end the program? (Enter yes or no):
yes
>>>
```

Step 18: When your Python code is complete and correct, copy and paste your work into a Word document. Save and print your document, then turn it in for grading.

Name: _____

Lab 5.5 – Programming Challenge 1: Yum Yum Burger Joint

For the following programming problem, write:
1. the algorithm
2. the pseudocode
3. the flowchart
4. Python code

Copy and paste your work into a Word document, labeling each section. Save and print your document, then turn it in for grading.

Yum Yum Burger Joint

Write a program that will calculate the cost of purchasing a meal. This program will include decisions and loops. Details of the program are as follows:

- Your menu items include only the following food at the indicated price:
  - Yum Yum Burger = .99
  - Grease Yum Fries = .79
  - Soda Yum = 1.09
- Allow the program user to purchase any quantity of these items in one order.
- Allow the program user to purchase one or more types of these items in one order.
- After the order is placed, calculate the total and add a 6% sales tax.
- Print to the screen a receipt showing the total purchase price.

Your sample output might look as follows:

```
Enter 1 for Yum Yum Burger
Enter 2 for Grease Yum Fries
Enter 3 for Soda Yum
Enter now ->1
Enter the number of burgers you want 3
Do you want to end your order? (Enter yes or no): no

Enter 1 for Yum Yum Burger
Enter 2 for Grease Yum Fries
Enter 3 for Soda Yum
Enter now ->3
Enter the number of sodas you want 2
Do you want to end your order? (Enter yes or no): no
```

```
Enter 1 for Yum Yum Burger
Enter 2 for Grease Yum Fries
Enter 3 for Soda Yum
Enter now ->1
Enter the number of burgers you want 1
Do you want to end your order? (Enter yes or no): no

Enter 1 for Yum Yum Burger
Enter 2 for Grease Yum Fries
Enter 3 for Soda Yum
Enter now ->2
Enter the number of fries you want 2
Do you want to end your order? (Enter yes or no): yes

The total price is $ 8.1832
Do you want to end program? (Enter no to process a new
order): no

Enter 1 for Yum Yum Burger
Enter 2 for Grease Yum Fries
Enter 3 for Soda Yum
Enter now ->2
Enter the number of fries you want 2
Do you want to end your order? (Enter yes or no): no

Enter 1 for Yum Yum Burger
Enter 2 for Grease Yum Fries
Enter 3 for Soda Yum
Enter now ->3
Enter the number of sodas you want 2
Do you want to end your order? (Enter yes or no): yes

The total price is $ 3.9856
Do you want to end program? (Enter no to process a new
order): yes
```

Lab 6: Repetition Structures II
This lab accompanies Chapter 5 of *Starting Out with Programming Logic & Design*.

Name: _____

Lab 6.1 – For Loop and Pseudocode

Critical Review

A counter-controlled loop iterates a specific number of times. Although you can write this with a while or a do-while loop as performed in Lab 5, most programming languages provide a loop known as the **for loop**. This loop is specifically designed as a counter-controlled loop.

The process of the for loop is:
- The loop keeps a count of the number of times that it iterates, and when the count reaches a specified amount, the loop stops.
- A counter-controlled loop uses a variable known as a counter variable to store the number of iterations that it has performed.
- Using the counter, the following three actions take place: initialization, test, and increment.

The pseudocode for a for statement looks as follows:

```
For counterVariable = startingValue to maxValue
     statement
     statement
     statement
     etc.
End For
```

This lab requires you to implement a counter-controlled loop using a for statement.

Step 1: Examine the following code.

```
Constant Integer MAX_HOURS = 24
Declare Integer hours

For hours = 1 to MAX_HOURS
     Display "The hour is ", hours
End For
```

99

Step 2: Explain what you think will be displayed to the screen in Step 1. (Reference For loop, p. 186):

_____

_____

_____

Step 3: Write a for loop that will print 60 minutes to the screen. Complete the missing lines of code.

```
Constant Integer MAX_MINUTES = _____
Declare Integer minutes

For _____ = 1 to _____
      Display _____
End For
```

Step 4: Write a for loop that will print 60 seconds to the screen. Complete the missing lines of code.

```
Constant Integer MAX_SECONDS = _____
Declare Integer seconds

For _____ = 1 to _____
      Display _____
End For
```

Step 5: For loops can also be used to increment by more than 1. Examine the following code.

```
Constant Integer MAX_VALUE = 10
Declare Integer counter

For counter = 0 to MAX_VALUE Step 2
      Display "The number is ", counter
End For
```

Step 6: Explain what you think will be displayed to the screen in Step 5. (Reference Incrementing by Values Other than 1, p. 190):

_____

_____

_____

Step 7: Write a for loop that will display the numbers starting at 20, then 40, then 60, and continuing the sequence all the way to 200.

```
Constant Integer MAX_VALUE = _____
Declare Integer counter


For counter = _____ to MAX_VALUE Step _____
      Display "The number is ", _____
End For
```

Step 8: For loops can also be used when the user controls the number of iterations. Examine the following code:

```
Declare Integer numStudents
Declare Integer counter

Display "Enter the number of students in class"
Input numStudents

For counter = 1 to numStudents
      Display "Student #", counter
End For
```

Step 9: Explain what you think will be displayed to the screen in Step 8. (Reference Letting the User Control the Number of Iterations, p. 194):

_____

_____

_____

Step 10: For loops are also commonly used to calculate a running total. Examine the following code.

```
Declare Integer counter
Declare Integer total = 0
Declare Integer number

For counter = 1 to 5
      Display "Enter a number: "
      Input number
      Set total = total + number
End For

Display "The total is: ", total
```

Step 11: Explain what you think will be displayed to the screen in Step 10. (Reference Calculating a Running Total, p. 201.):

_____

_____

_____

Step 12: Write missing lines for a program that allows the user to enter as many ages as they wish and then find the average.

```
Declare Integer counter
Declare Integer totalAge = 0
Declare Real averageAge = 0
Declare Integer age
Declare Integer number

Display "How many ages do you want to enter: "

Input _____

For counter = 1 to number
      Display "Enter age: "

      Input _____

      Set totalAge = _____ + _____
End For

averageAge = _____ / _____

Display "The average age is ", _____
```

Name: _____

Lab 6.2 – For Loop and Flowcharts

Critical Review

A flowchart for a for loop is similar to that of a while loop, where a condition controls the iterations. Here is an example of a for loop using a flowcharting tool such as Visio.

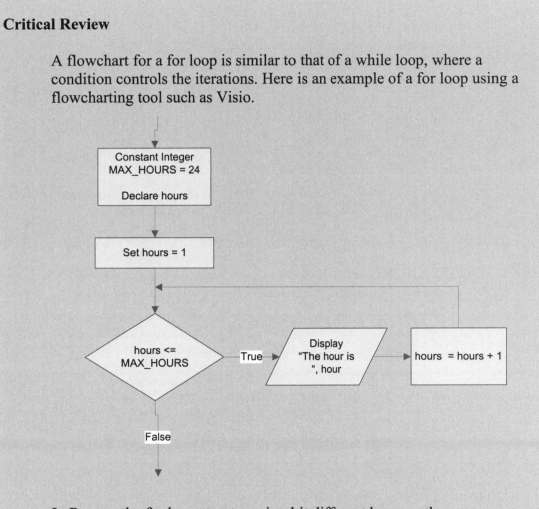

In Raptor, the for loop structures is a bit different because the programmer has less control over the loop symbol. Notice these differences in the following flowchart:

a. The variables are still declared and initialized to the same starting values.
b. The condition is now `hours > MAX_HOURS` rather than `hours <= MAX_HOURS`. This is done because in Raptor, False or No statements continue the code and True or Yes statements end the code. This is the opposite as demonstrated in the textbook.
c. The code within the loop is the same.

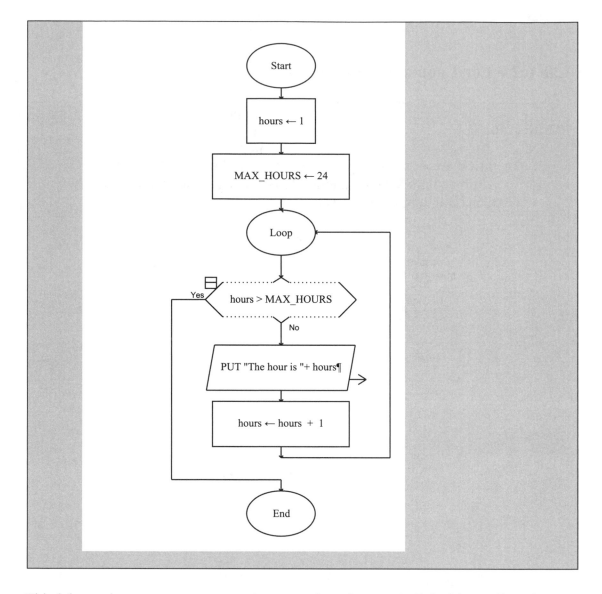

This lab requires you to convert various pseudocode steps in Lab 6.1 to a flowchart. Use an application such as Raptor or Visio. These instructors assume you are using Raptor.

The Seconds Counter
Step 1: Start Raptor and save your document as *Lab 6-2Seconds*. The *.rap* file extension will be added automatically.

Step 2: The first loop to code is the pseudocode from Step 4, Lab 6.1. This loop will print 60 seconds to the screen. The complete pseudocode is below:

```
Constant Integer MAX_SECONDS = 60
Declare Integer seconds
```

```
For seconds = 1 to 60
      Display "The second is ", seconds
End For
```

Step 3: Click the Loop symbol and add it between the Start and the End symbol. Above the Loop symbol, add two assignment statements. Set a variable named seconds to 1 and a variable named MAX_SECONDS to 60.

Step 4: Double-click the Diamond symbol and add the condition that will execute the loop through 60 iterations.

Step 5: Add an output statement if the loop is NO. This statement will display the seconds variable to the screen.

Step 6: Add an assignment statement next that will increment the seconds variable by 1.

Step 7: Execute your flowchart to see if your output matches the following. If not, repeat the steps to identify the error and execute again.

```
The second is 1
The second is 2
The second is 3
     .....Continues from 4 to 57......
The second is 58
The second is 59
The second is 60
----Run finished----
```

Step 8: Copy and paste your flowchart into a Word document. Label it The Seconds Counter. Save and print your document.

The Accumulator

Step 1: Start Raptor and save your document as *Lab 6-2Accumulator*. The *.rap* file extension will be added automatically.

Step 2: The next loop to code is the pseudocode from Step 10, Lab 6.1. This loop will take in a number and accumulate the total. The complete pseudocode is below:

```
Declare Integer counter
Declare Integer total = 0
Declare Integer number

For counter = 1 to 5
```

```
            Display "Enter a number: "
            Input number
            Set total = total + number
      End For

      Display "The total is total: ", total
```

Step 3: Click the Loop symbol and add it between the Start and the End symbol. Above the Loop symbol, add three assignment statements. Set a variable named counter to 1, a variable named total to 0, and a variable named number to 0.

Step 4: Double-click the Diamond symbol and add the condition that will execute the loop through 5 iterations.

Step 5: Add an input statement if the loop is NO. This statement will ask the user to enter a number.

Step 6: Add an assignment statement that will accumulate the total such as total = total + number.

Step 7: Add an assignment statement that will increment the counter variable by 1.

Step 8: Add an output statement outside of the loop if the condition is YES. This should display total.

Step 9: Execute your flowchart to see if your output matches the following. If not, repeat the steps to identify the error and execute again.

Input values are:
```
13
23
24
52
18
```

The expected output is:
```
The total is 130
----Run finished----
```

Step 10: Copy and paste your flowchart into a Word document. Label it The Accumulator. Save and print your document.

The Average Age
Step 1: Start Raptor and save your document as *Lab 6-2AverageAge*. The *.rap* file extension will be added automatically.

Step 2: The next loop to code is the pseudocode from Step 12, Lab 6.1. This loop will take in various amounts of ages and then find the average. The complete pseudocode is below:

```
Declare Integer counter
Declare Integer totalAge = 0
Declare Real averageAge = 0
Declare Integer age
Declare Integer number

Display "How many ages do you want to enter: "
Input number

For counter = 1 to number
     Display "Enter age: "
     Input age
     Set totalAge = totalAge + age
End For

averageAge = totalAge / number

Display "The average age is ", averageAge
```

Step 3: Click the Loop symbol and add it between the Start and the End symbol. Above the Loop symbol, add five assignment statements. Set counter to 1, totalAge to 0, averageAge to 0, age to 0, and number to 0.

Step 4: Above the Loop symbol, add an Input symbol that asks the user how many ages they want to enter. Store the answer in the number variable.

Step 5: Double-click the Diamond symbol and add the condition that will execute the loop as long as number is less than counter. This can be written as counter > number.

Step 6: Add an input statement if the loop is NO. This statement will ask the user to enter an age.

Step 7: Add an assignment statement that will accumulate the totalAge.

Step 8: Add an assignment statement that will increment the counter variable by 1.

Step 9: Add an assignment statement outside of the loop if the condition is YES. This should calculate the averageAge as averageAge = totalAge / number.

Step 10: Add an output statement outside of the loop if the condition is YES. This should display averageAge.

Step 11: Execute your flowchart to see if your output matches the following. If not, repeat the steps to identify the error and execute again.

Input values are:
```
4 - how many ages to enter

45
67
34
27
```

The expected output is:
```
The average age is 43.2500
----Run finished----
```

Step 12: Copy and paste your flowchart into a Word document. Label it The Average Age. Save and print your document.

Name: _____

Lab 6.3 – Python Code

Critical Review

You use the for statement to write a counter-controlled loop. In Python, the for statement is designed to work with a sequence of data items. When the statement executes, it iterates once for each item in the sequence. The general format is a follows:

```
for variable in [value1, value2, etc.]:
    statement
    statement
    etc.
```

Using the range function

When it is too cumbersome to print all the values to be displayed, you can use Python's range function. If you pass one argument to the range function, that argument is used as the ending limit of the list. If you pass two arguments to the range function, the first argument is used as the starting value of the list and the second argument is used as the ending limit. Here are two examples:

| ```
for num in range(5):
    print num
```<br><br>This code will display the following:<br><br>0<br>1<br>2<br>3<br>4 | ```
for num in range(1, 5):
    print num
```<br><br>This code will display the following:<br><br>1<br>2<br>3<br>4 |
|---|---|

Letting the User Control the Number of Iterations

Sometimes the programmer needs to let the user control the number of times that a loop iterates. This is done by first letting the user enter how many times they want their loop to execute. Then, the range function is used to control the iterations. It is important to use the starting value of 0 for the loop to execute the exact number of times. The general format is as follows:

```
number = input('How many iterations do you want: ')

for counter in range(0, number):
        Statements…
        Statements…
```

The goal of this lab is to convert all flowcharts in Lab 6.2 to Python code.

Step 1: Start the IDLE Environment for Python. Prior to entering code, save your file by clicking on File and then Save. Select your location and save this file as *Lab6-3.py*. Be sure to include the .py extension.

Step 2: Document the first few lines of your program to include your name, the date, and a brief description of what the program does.

Step 3: Start your program with the following code for main:

```
#Lab 6-3 Practicing for loops

#the main function
def main():

    #A Basic For loop


    #The Second Counter code


    #The Accumulator code


    #The Average Age code

#calls main
main()
```

Step 4: Under the documentation for A Basic For Loop, add the following lines of code:

```
print 'I will display the numbers 1 through 5.'
for num in [1, 2, 3, 4, 5]:
        print num
```

On the first iteration, 1 is placed into the variable num and num is then printed to the screen. The process is continued as follows:

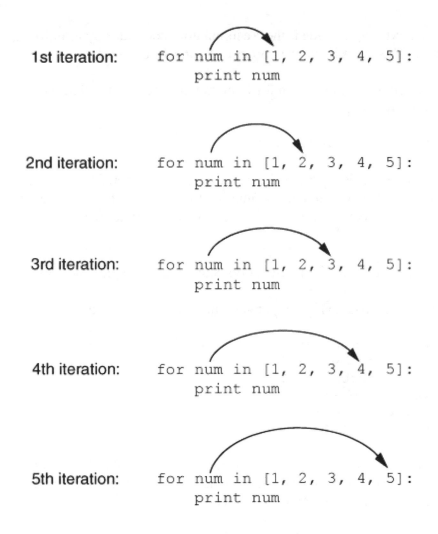

```
1st iteration:     for num in [1, 2, 3, 4, 5]:
                       print num


2nd iteration:     for num in [1, 2, 3, 4, 5]:
                       print num


3rd iteration:     for num in [1, 2, 3, 4, 5]:
                       print num


4th iteration:     for num in [1, 2, 3, 4, 5]:
                       print num


5th iteration:     for num in [1, 2, 3, 4, 5]:
                       print num
```

Execute your program. Notice that the output is as follows:

```
>>>
I will display the numbers 1 through 5.
1
2
3
4
5
>>>
```

Step 5: The next loop to code is the Second Counter code. This loop can be processed in the same way as Step 4; however, it would take a long time to write 1 through 60 in the for loop definition. Therefore, the `range` function should be used to simplify the process. Write a for loop that has a range from 1 to 61. If you stop at 60, only 59 seconds will be printed. If you only provide one argument, the starting value will be 0. (Reference the Critical Review section above for the exact syntax.)

Step 6: The next loop to code is the Accumulator code. Start by initializing a total variable to 0. This must be done in order to accumulate values.

Step 7: The next step is to write a for loop that iterates 5 times. The easiest way to do this is the following.

```
for counter in range(5):
```

Step 8: Inside the for loop, allow the user to enter a number. Then, add an accumulation statement that adds the number to total. In Python, the range function determines the number of iterations, so it is not necessary to manually increment counter.

Step 9: Outside of the for loop, use a print statement to display the total.

Step 10: Compare your sample input and output to the following:

```
Enter a number: 54
Enter a number: 32
Enter a number: 231
Enter a number: 23
Enter a number: 87
The total is 427
```

Step 11: The final loop to code is the Average Age code. Start by initializing totalAge and averageAge to 0. (Reference the Critical Review section above on Letting the User Control the Number of Iterations).

Step 12: The next step is to ask how many ages the user wants to enter. Store the answer in the number variable.

Step 13: Write the definition for the for loop using the range function such as:

```
for counter in range(0, number):
```

Step 14: Inside the for loop, allow the user to enter an age.

Step 15: Inside the for loop, add the code that will accumulate age into the totalAge variable.

Step 16: Outside of the loop, calculate the averageAge as averageAge = totalAge / number.

Step 17: Outside of the loop, display the averageAge variable to the screen.

Step 18: Compare your sample input and output to the following:

```
How many ages do you want to enter: 6
Enter an age: 13
Enter an age: 43
Enter an age: 25
Enter an age: 34
Enter an age: 28
Enter an age: 43
The average age is 31
>>>
```

Step 18: Execute your program so that all loops work. When your Python code is complete and correct, copy and paste your work into a Word document. Save and print your document, then turn it in for grading.

Name: _____

Lab 6.4 – Programming Challenge 1: Average Test Scores

For the following programming problem, write:
1. the algorithm
2. the pseudocode
3. the flowchart
4. Python code

Copy and paste your work into a Word document, labeling each section. Save and print your document, then turn it in for grading.

Average Test Scores

Write a program that will allow a teacher to calculate the average test score for a certain number of students. The teacher can enter the number of students who took the test, and then the score for each student. Your program will then calculate the average score and print out the results. Your program must use appropriate loop, modules, and run multiple times for different sets of test scores.

Your sample output might look as follows:

```
How many students took the test: 9
Enter their score: 98
Enter their score: 78
Enter their score: 99
Enter their score: 92
Enter their score: 87
Enter their score: 100
Enter their score: 88
Enter their score: 81
Enter their score: 79
The average test score is 89
Do you want to end program? (Enter no to process a new
set of scores): yes
```

Lab 7: Functions

This lab accompanies Chapter 6 of *Starting Out with Programming Logic & Design*.

Name: _____

Lab 7.1 – Functions and Pseudocode

Critical Review

You have been coding with modules in pseudocode and functions when using Python. Your modules in pseudocode can be made into functions by returning a value.

A **function** is a special type of module that returns a value back to the part of the program that called it.

Most programming languages provide a library of prewritten functions that perform commonly needed tasks. Library functions are built into the programming language and you can call them as needed.

Writing Your Own Function that Returns an Integer
Step 1: A function contains three parts; a header, a body, and a return statement. The function header specifies the data type of the value that is to returned, the name of the function, and any parameter variables used by the function to accept arguments. The body is comprised of one or more statements that are executed when the function is called.

Complete the following:
(Reference Writing Your Own Functions, p. 225).

   a. Write a function with the header named addTen.
   b. The function will accept an Integer variable named number.
   c. The function body will ask the user to enter a number and the add 10 to the number. The answer will be stored in the variable number.
   d. The return statement will return the value of number.

```
Function a._____   a._____   (b._____)
      Display "Enter a number:"
      Input c._____
      Set c._____ = number + 10
Return d._____
```

Step 2: In the following space, write a function call to your function from Step 1.

```
Set number =  _____  (_____)
```

Writing Your Own Function that Returns a Boolean Value
Step 1: A Boolean function will return a value of either true or false. You can use these functions to test a condition. They are useful for simplifying complex conditions that are tested in decision and repetition structures.

Complete the following:
(Reference Returning Boolean Values, p. 238).

    a.   Write a function with the header named gender.
    b.   The function will accept a Boolean variable named answer.
    c.   The function body will ask the user to enter their gender into the variable type and then determine if they are male or female with an if statement.
    d.   The return statement will return the value of answer.

```
Function a._____   a._____   (b._____)
        Declare String type
        Display "Enter your gender (male or female):"

        Input c._____

        If (c._____ == "male") then
              answer = False
        Else
              answer = True
        End If

Return d._____
```

Step 2: In the following space, write a function call to your function from Step 1.

```
Set answer =  _____  (_____)
```

Using Mathematical Library Function: sqrt
Step 1: The sqrt function accepts an argument and returns the square root of the argument.

Complete the following:
(Reference The sqrt Function, p. 240).

    a.   Declare a variable named myNumber and a variable named squareRoot of the data type Real.

b. Ask the user to enter a number they want to find the square root of. Store the input in myNumber.
c. Call the sqrt function to determine the square root of myNumber.
d. Display the square root to the screen.

```
Declare Integer a._____

Declare Real a._____

Display "Enter a number:"

Input b._____

Set c. _____ = _____

Display "The square root is", d._____
```

Using Formatting Functions

Step 1: Most languages provide one or more functions that format numbers in some way. A common use of these functions is to format numbers as currency amounts. While a specific programming language will have its own name for formatting currency, use the function currencyFormat for pseudocode.

Complete the following:
(Reference Formatting Functions, p. 246).

a. Declare a variable named subtotal, a constant variable named tax set to the rate of .06, and a variable named total.
b. Ask the user to enter the subtotal. Store the input in subtotal.
c. Calculate the total as subtotal + subtotal * tax.
d. Make a call to the currencyFormat function and pass it total. Since you are not displaying it on this line, simply set the return value to total.
e. Display the total to the screen.

```
Declare Real a._____

Declare Constant Real a._____

Declare Real a._____

Display "Enter the subtotal:"

Input b._____

Set c._____ = _____

total = d._____ (_____)

Display "The total is $", e._____
```

Name: _____

Lab 7.2 – Functions and Flowcharts

Critical Review

When creating a flowchart for a program that has functions, you draw a separate flowchart for each function.

The starting terminal symbol usually shows the name of the function, along with any parameters that the function has.

The ending terminal symbol reads Return, followed by the value or expression being returned.

In Raptor, built-in procedures and functions perform a wide variety of tasks on the programmer's behalf, saving development time and reducing the chance for errors. Raptor built-in functions can return values, but modules made by the user do not have that ability.

Raptor has the following built-in functions.
basic math: `rem, mod, sqrt, log, abs, ceiling, floor`
trigonometry: `sin, cos, tan, cot, arcsin, arcos, arctan, arccot`
miscellaneous: `random, Length_of`

If you want to learn what each of these functions does, use the Help menu in Raptor and search for the function name.

While `ceiling` and `floor` round a number to the nearest integer, there is no function in Raptor that will round a number just to two decimal places.

The `random` function in Raptor takes no arguments. To generate a random integer from 1 to n, use `floor((random*n) + 1)`. For example, you can simulate the roll of a die (random number from 1 to 6) with `floor((random * 6) + 1)`.

This lab requires you to create the flowchart from p. 222 of your textbook on Using Random Numbers using the RANDOM function. Use an application such as Raptor or Visio. These instructions assume you are using Raptor.

Step 1: Start by reading the pseudocode on pp. 221 and 222 of your textbook on Using Random Numbers. In addition to simply displaying the random values, your program will also meet the following requirements:

- Allow the two players of the dice game to enter their names in variables named playerOne and playerTwo.
- Based on the random roll of the dice, your program will determine which value is higher or if they tie, and declare one player a winner.
- Create structure in your program by creating the following modules:
  - o An inputNames( ) module that will ask the players to enter their names
  - o A rollDice( ) module that will call the RANDOM function and determine the winner. This will be done with a decision statement.
  - o A displayInfo( ) module that will print the winner's name to the screen.
- Additionally, your program should allow the same two players to play as many times as they want.

Step 2: Start Raptor and save your document as *Lab 7-2*. The *.rap* file extension will be added automatically.

Step 3: Start by adding a comment box with the necessary variables.

Step 4: Add your loop to run multiple times and your module calls in the main module. Your flowchart might look as follows:

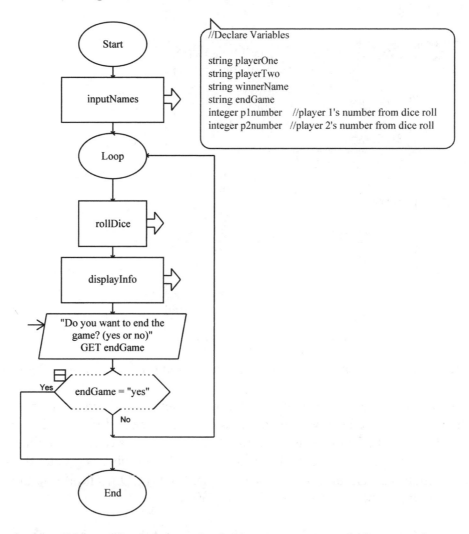

Step 5: Code the inputNames( ) module so both players can enter their names into the appropriate variable.

Step 6: Go to the rollDice( ) module and add an assignment statement. Assign p1number to whatever the RANDOM function return. The assignment box input box should look like this:

Step 7: Add a second assignment statement and do the same for p2number.

Step 8: Add a selection statement that will determine which number is larger, or if there is a tie. The best way to do this is to create a nested if-else where you first check to see if p1number is equal to p2number. If so, assign winnerName equal to "TIE." If not, create a second decision to see if p1number is greater than p2number. If so, then winnerName should be set equal to playerOne and if not, then winnerName should be set equal to playerTwo.

Step 9: Go to the displayInfo( ) module and print the winner's name to the screen.

Step 10: Copy and paste your flowchart into a Word document. Save and print your document, then turn it in for grading.

Name: _____

Lab 7.3 – Python Code and Random

Critical Review

A value-returning function is a function that returns a value back to the part of the program that called it. In Python, you have been using functions that return values and those that do not.

Recall the function calls from Lab 6-4. The first call returns number back to the number variable. The second call just displays a value and there is no need to return a value.

```
number = getNumber(number)  #value returning function
printAverage(averageScores) #function returns no value
```

Standard Library Functions

Python comes with a *standard library* of functions that have already been written for you. These functions, known as *library functions,* make a programmer's job easier because they perform many of the tasks that programmers commonly need to perform. In fact, you have already used several of Python's library functions. Some of the functions that you have used are input, raw_input, and range. Python has many other library functions.

The random Function

In order to use the random function in Python, you must import the random library. This loads the library into memory so that you can use the functions that exist within it. To do this, simply add the following line to the top of your code:

```
import random
```

One function in the random library is the random.randint( ) module. This module accepts two arguments; the first is the starting number and the second is the ending number. Here is how you would get a random number between 1 and 6:

```
p1number = random.randint(1, 6)
```

Writing Your Own Value-Returning Functions

We have already written our own value-returning functions that return one variable to the place where the function was called.

However, you can also return more than one value in Python. The function call might look as follows:

```
playerOne, playerTwo = inputNames(playerOne, playerTwo)
```

The return statement looks as follows:

```
return playerOne, playerTwo
```

Formatting Numbers

To format a real number to a specific decimal range, use the % symbol. For example, *print 'Money due is %.2f'% (moneyDue)*

The goal of this lab is to convert the Dice Game in Lab 7.2 to Python code.

Step 1: Start the IDLE Environment for Python. Prior to entering code, save your file by clicking on File and then Save. Select your location and save this file as *Lab7-3.py*. Be sure to include the .py extension.

Step 2: Document the first few lines of your program to include your name, the date, and a brief description of what the program does.

Step 3: Start your program with the following code for main:

```
#Lab 7-3 The Dice Game
#add libraries needed

#the main function
def main():
    print
    #initialize variables


    #call to inputNames

    #while loop to run program again
    while endProgram == 'no':

        #initialize variables

        #call to rollDice

        #call to displayInfo


        endProgram = raw_input('Do you want to end
program? (Enter yes or no): ')


#this function gets the players names


#this function will get the random values


#this function displays the winner


# calls main
main()
```

Step 4: Under the documentation for adding libraries, add the following statement:

```
import random
```

Step 5: Under the documentation for initialize variables, set endProgram to 'no' and playerOne and playerTwo to 'NO NAME'.

Step 6: Under the documentation for making a call to inputNames, set the function call to both playerOne and playerTwo and pass both variables to the function as arguments. This must be done because both values need to be returned from the function. This is done as follows:

```
playerOne, playerTwo = inputNames(playerOne, playerTwo)
```

Step 7: Inside your while loop, set winnersName to 'NO NAME' and p1number and p2number to 0.

Step 8: Make a call to rollDice and pass the necessary variables needed in this function. This function should be set to the winnerName as that variable will be returned from the function. This is done as follows:

```
winnerName = rollDice(p1number, p2number, playerOne,
playerTwo, winnerName)
```

Step 9: Make a call to displayInfo and pass it winnerName.

Step 10: The next step is to write the function that will allow both players to enter their names. Write a function header that matches your function call in Step 6, making sure to accept two arguments. The body of this function will use the raw_input function to take in both players' names, and one return statement that returns both playerOne and playerTwo variables. The return statement should look as follows:

```
return playerOne, playerTwo
```

Step 11: The next function to code is the rollDice function. Write the function header to match the function call in Step 8. This function body will call the random function to determine p1number and p2number. The code should look like this:

```
p1number = random.randint(1, 6)
p2number = random.randint(1, 6)
```

Step 12: Next, inside this function write a nested if-else statement that will set winnerName to playerOne name, playerTwo name, or "TIE."
Step 13: The final step in this function is to return winnerName.

Step 14: The final function to code is the displayInfo function. Write the function header to match the call made in Step 9. The body of the function should simply print the winnerName variable to the screen.

Step 15: Execute your program so that all loops work. When your Python code is complete and correct, copy and paste your work into a Word document. Save and print your document, then turn it in for grading.

Name:_____

Lab 7.4 – Python Code and Formatting

Critical Review

Formatting Numbers
If you need to format a real number to a specific decimal range, use the % symbol. For example:
print 'Money due is %.2f'% (moneyDue)

The goal of this lab is to practice formatting numbers in Python code.

Step 1: Start the IDLE Environment for Python. Open up *Lab6-4.py* that calculated the average test scores. Prior to entering code, save your file as *Lab7-4.py* by clicking on File and then Save As. Select your location and save this file as *Lab7-4.py*. Be sure to include the .py extension.

Step 2: Run your program with the following input values:

```
How many students took the test: 5
Enter their score: 97
Enter their score: 93
Enter their score: 87
Enter their score: 72
Enter their score: 84
```

Step 3: The problem with the output is that by default, Python simply truncates any decimal value that the calculated answer may have. Notice the output is as follows:

```
The average test score is 86
```

The correct average should be 86.6.

Step 4: In your printAverage( ) module, change the print statement to the following:

```
print 'The average test score is %.2f'%(averageScores)
```

Step 5: Run your program again with the same input values from Step 2. Copy your output into a Word document.

Step 6: You will notice that the output just simply prints the two decimal places of .00 and still not the correct value of 86.6. This is because the previous variables are assumed to be integers. To correct this, go to the getAverage function and change the formula to convert totalScores to a float. The formula should now read:

```
averageScores = float(totalScores)/ number
```

Step 7: Run your program again with the same input values from Step 2. Copy your output values into your Word document under the values from Step 5. Save and print.

Name: _____

Lab 7.5 – Programming Challenge 1: Math Problems

For the following programming problem, write:
1. the algorithm
2. the pseudocode
3. the flowchart
4. Python code

Copy and paste your work into a Word document, labeling each section. Save and print your document, then turn it in for grading.

Math Problems

Write a program that will ask a student to enter his or her name and then to solve 10 mathematical equations. The program should display two random numbers for the student to add, such as:

```
  247
+ 129
```

The program should allow the student to enter the answer. The program should then display whether the answer was right or wrong, and accumulate number of the correct answers. After the 10 questions are answered, calculate the average correct. Then display the student name, the number right, and the average right both in decimal and percentage format.

In addition to any system functions you may use, you might consider the following functions:
- A function that allows the student to enter his or her name.
- A function that gets two random numbers, anywhere from 1 to 500.
- A function that displays the equation and asks the user to enter the answer.
- A function that checks to see if the answer is right and accumulates the number of correct answers.
- A function that calculates the results.
- A function that displays the student name, the number right, and the average right.

Your sample output might look as follows (random numbers will be different):

```
Enter Student Name: Katie
What is the answer to the following equation?
```

```
424
+
28
What is the sum: 472
Wrong

What is the answer to the following equation?
163
+
233
What is the sum: 396
Right

What is the answer to the following equation?
285
+
453
What is the sum: 688
Wrong
```

(Etc. through 10 iterations)

```
Information for student: Katie
The number right: 5
The average right is 0.50 or 50.0 %
```

Lab 8: Input Validation
This lab accompanies Chapter 7 of *Starting Out with Programming Logic & Design*.

Name: _____

Lab 8.1 – Input Validation

Critical Review

If a computer reads bad data as input, it will produce bad data as output. Programs should be designed to reject bad data that is given as input.

Garbage in, garbage out (GIGO) refers to the fact that computers cannot tell the difference between good data and bad data without programming. Discerning good data from bad is called **validation**.

Both numbers and strings can be validated.

The goal of this lab is to identify potential errors with algorithms and programs you have already coded.

Step 1: Imagine a program that calls for the user to enter a password of at least 8 alphanumeric characters. Identify at least two potential input errors.

_____

_____

Step 2: Imagine a program that calls for the user to enter patients' blood pressure. Blood pressure ranges are between 50 and 230. Identify at least two potential input errors.

_____

_____

Step 3: Open up either your Lab 5-3.rap flowchart or your Lab 5-4.py Python code. This program allowed the user to enter in 7 days' worth of bottle returns and then calculated the average. Examine the program and identify at least two potential input errors.

_____

_____

Step 4: Open up either your Lab 6-4.rap flowchart or your Lab 6-4.py Python code. This program allowed a teacher to enter any number of test scores and then calculated the average score. Examine the program and identify at least two potential input errors.

_____

_____

Name: _____

Lab 8.2 – Input Validation and Pseudocode

Critical Review

> **Input validation** is commonly done with a loop that iterates as long as an input variable contains bad data. Either a posttest or a pretest loop will work. If you want to also display an error message, use a pretest loop, otherwise, a posttest loop will work.
>
> Functions are often used for complex validation code.

The goal of this lab is to write input validation pseudocode.

Step 1: Examine the following main module from Lab 5.2. Notice that if the user enters a capital 'Y,' the program will end because the while loop only checks for a lower case 'y.'

```
Module main ()

        //Step 1: Declare variables below
        Declare Integer totalBottles = 0
        Declare Integer counter = 1
        Declare Integer todayBottles = 0
        Declare Real totalPayout
        Declare String keepGoing = 'y'

        //Step 3: Loop to run program again
        While keepGoing == 'y'
            //Step 2: Call functions
            getBottles(totalBottles, todayBottles,
            counter)
            calcPayout(totalBottles, totalPayout)
            printInfo(totalBottles, totalPayout)

            Display "Do you want to run the program
            again? (Enter y for yes or n for no.)"
            Input keepGoing
        End While
End Module
```

Step 2: Write a line of code that will convert the input value to a lowercase value. (See Validating String Input, p. 264.)

_____

_____

Step 3: Examine the getBottles module from the same program. Notice the potential input error of the user entering a negative value into todayBottles. Rewrite the module with an input validation loop inside the existing while loop that will verify that the entry into todayBottles is greater than 0. If the user enters a 0 or negative value, display an error message. (Reference Input Validation Loop, p. 258.)

Previous Code

```
//getBottles module
Module getBottles(Integer totalBottles, Integer
todayBottles, Integer counter)
    While counter <=7
        Display "Enter number of bottles returned for
        the day:"
        Input todayBottles
        totalBottles = totalBottles + todayBottles
        counter = counter + 1
    End While
End Module
```

Validation Code

```
//getBottles module
Module getBottles(Integer totalBottles, Integer
todayBottles, Integer counter)
    While counter <=7
```

_____

_____

_____


```
        Display "Enter number of bottles
        returned for the day:"
        Input todayBottles
```

_____

```
            totalBottles = totalBottles + todayBottles
            counter = counter + 1
        End While
End Module
```

Step 4: Examine the following pseudocode from Lab 6.4. Rewrite the module with a validation loop so that no fewer than 2 students and no more than 30 students take the test.

Previous Code

```
Module getNumber(Integer Ref number)
        Display "How many students took the test: "
        Input number
End Module
```

Validated Code

```
Module getNumber(Integer Ref number)
```

_____

_____

_____

_____

_____

_____

```
End Module
```

Step 5: Examine the following pseudocode from Lab 6.4. Rewrite the module with a validation loop so that the test score must be between 0 and 100.

Previous Code

```
Module getScores(Real Ref totalScores, Integer number,
Real score, Integer counter)
        For counter = 1 to number
            Display "Enter their score:"
            Input score
            Set totalScores = totalScores + score
        End For
End Module
```

Validated Code

```
Module getScores(Real Ref totalScores, Integer number,
Real score, Integer counter)
```

_____

_____

_____

_____

_____

_____

```
End Module
```

Name: _____

Lab 8.3 – Functions and Flowcharts

Critical Review

Based on the type of loop used for validation, you may have noticed the concept of a **priming read**. This is the first input before the validation loop. Its purpose is to get the first input value that will be tested by the validation loop.

A priming read is used with a while loop, rather than with a do-while loop.

Note: If the programmer asks for a particular type of input (either numeric or string), the user is free to enter something else. This will normally cause a fatal error at some point in the program execution. Avoiding these fatal errors is beyond the scope of basic Raptor programming. What this means is that all errors cannot be resolved using Raptor.

This lab requires you to modify the flowchart from Lab 6-4.rap to incorporate validation loops. Use an application such as Raptor or Visio. These instructions assume you are using Raptor.

Step 1: Start Raptor and open your flowchart from Lab 6-4.rap. Go to File and then Save As and save your document as *Lab 8-3*. The *.rap* file extension will be added automatically.

Step 2: In the main module, modify your loop condition so that the user must enter a "yes" or a "no" value. This can be done with nested Loop symbols. Your flowchart might look as follows:

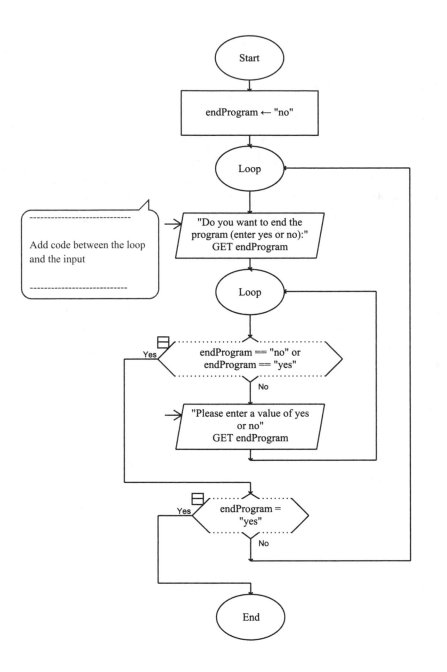

Step 3: In the getNumber module, modify the code so that the input must be at least 2 and no more than 30 students. If the user enters a valid number, the program should continue. If not, display an error message that says, "Please enter a number between 2 and 30 – Try again!!" Use a prime read in this situation.

Copy your getNumber module flowchart into a Word document.

Step 4: In the getScores module, modify the code so that the input must be between 0 and 100. If the user enters a valid number, the program should continue. If not, display an error message that says, "Please enter a number between 0 and 100 – Try again!!" Use a prime read in this situation. Paste your getScores module flowchart into your Word document from Step 3. Save and print.

Name: _____

Lab 8.4 – Python Code and Input Validation

Critical Review

Numeric validation loops in Python are done by writing the types of loops you already are familiar with. Code using a prime read might look as follows:

```
number = input('Enter a number between 1 and 10: ')
    while number < 1 or number > 10:
        print 'Please enter a number between 1 and 10'
        number = input('Enter a number between 1 and 10: ')
```

String input validation code uses the not keyword to check the opposite of something. Code using a prime read might look as follows:

```
endProgram = raw_input('Do you want to end program?
(Enter no or yes): ')
        while not (endProgram == 'yes' or endProgram
        == 'no'):
            print 'Please enter a yes or no'
            endProgram = raw_input('Do you want to end
            program? (Enter no to process a new set of
            scores): ')
```

The goal of this lab is to convert the Test Average program in Lab 8.3 to Python code.

Step 1: Start the IDLE Environment for Python. Open your Lab6-4.py program and click on File and then Save As. Select your location and save this file as *Lab*8-4.*py*. Be sure to include the .py extension.

Step 2: Modify the documentation in the first few lines of your program to include your name, the date, and a brief description of what the program does to include validation.

Step 3: Modify the main function so that the user must enter either a 'yes' or 'no' value in order for the loop to continue. Use a prime read and a while loop with an error message if a bad number is entered.

143

Step 4: Modify the getNumber function so that the user must enter a number between 2 and 30. Use a prime read and a while loop with an error message if a bad number is entered.

Step 5: Modify the getScores function so that the user must enter a number between 0 and 100. Use a prime read and a while loop with an error message if a bad number is entered.

Step 6: Execute your program so that all error code works. When your Python code is complete and correct, copy and paste your work into a Word document. Save and print your document, then turn it in for grading.

Name: _____

Lab 8.5 – Programming Challenge 1: Cell Phone Minute Calculator

For the following programming problem, write:
1. the algorithm
2. the pseudocode
3. the flowchart
4. Python code

Copy and paste your work into a Word document, labeling each section. Save and print your document, then turn it in for grading.

Cell Phone Minute Calculator

Design and write a program that calculates and displays the number of minutes over the monthly contract minutes that a cell phone user incurred. The program should ask the user how many minutes were used during the month and how many minutes were allowed. Validate the input as follows:

- The minimum minutes allowed should be at least 200, but not greater than 800. Validate input so that the minutes allowed are between 200 and 800.
- The minutes used must be over 0. Validate input so that the user does not enter a negative value.

Once correct data is entered, the program should calculate the number of minutes over the minutes allowed. If minutes were *not* over, print a message that they were not over the limit. If minutes were over, for every minute over, a .20 fee should be added to the monthly contract rate of 74.99. Be sure not to add the .20/minute fee for minutes 1 to the number of minutes allowed, but rather just for minutes over. Display the number of minutes used, minutes allowed, the number of minutes over, and the total due that month.

You might consider the following functions:
- Allows the user to enter minutes allowed within the range 200-800.
- Allows the user to enter the minutes used greater than or equal to 0.
- Calculates the total due and the total minutes over.
- Prints a monthly use report.

Your sample output might look as follows (note the validation code):

Sample 1 Showing Validation:

```
How many minutes are allowed: 1000
Please enter minutes between 200 and 800
How many minutes are allowed: 801
Please enter minutes between 200 and 800
How many minutes are allowed: 350
How many minutes were used: -10
Please enter minutes used of at least 0
How many minutes were used: 400

You were over your minutes by 50.

---------------MONTHLY USE REPORT------------------

Minutes allowed were 350
Minutes used were 400
Minutes over were 50
Total due is $ 84.99

Do you want to end program? (Enter no or yes): NO
Please enter a yes or no
Do you want to end program? (Enter no or yes): 9
Please enter a yes or no
Do you want to end program? (Enter no or yes): no
```

Sample 2 Showing Minutes Over:

```
How many minutes are allowed: 600
How many minutes were used: 884

You were over your minutes by 284.

---------------MONTHLY USE REPORT------------------

Minutes allowed were 600
Minutes used were 884
Minutes over were 284
Total due is $ 131.79

Do you want to end program? (Enter no or yes): no
```

Sample 3 Showing Minutes Not Over:

```
How many minutes are allowed: 400
How many minutes were used: 379

You were not over your minutes for the month.

---------------MONTHLY USE REPORT-----------------

Minutes allowed were 400
Minutes used were 379
Minutes over were 0
Total due is $ 74.99

Do you want to end program? (Enter no or yes): yes
```

Lab 9: Arrays

This lab accompanies Chapter 8 of *Starting Out with Programming Logic & Design.*

Name: _____

Lab 9.1 – Arrays and Pseudocode

Critical Review

An **array** allows you to store a group of items of the same data type together in memory.

A variable stores just a single value, and oftentimes they can be cumbersome to work with when your program has similar values.

Values stored in an array are called **elements**. Each element has a subscript that makes it unique.

An array is defined as follows:

```
Declare Integer numbers[10]
```

`Integer` defines the type of numbers that can be stored, `numbers` is the name of the array, and `[10]` is how many numbers can be stored.

In most languages, the first element is assigned the subscript of 0, so the above array actually runs from 0 to 9.

Constant variables can also be used to declare the size of an array.

```
Constant Integer SIZE = 5
Declare Integer numbers[SIZE] = 847, 1238, 48, 123, 840
```

Elements in the array

↓

847	1238	48	123	840
0	1	2	3	4

↑

Subscript or Index starting at 0

Loops are generally used to step through an array. This can be done using any type of loop and for any process such as filling, calculating, searching, sorting, or outputting elements of the array.

This lab examines the various ways of working with arrays by writing pseudocode. Read the following problem prior to completing the lab.

The American Red Cross wants you to write a program that will calculate the average pints of blood donated during a blood drive. The program should take in the number of pints donated, based on a seven-hour drive period. The average pints donated during that period should be calculated and displayed. Additionally, the highest and the lowest number of pints donated should be determined and displayed. Write a loop around the program to run multiple times.

Step 1: Declare the following variables:

- An array named pints of the data type Real of size 7
- A variable named totalPints of the data type Real
- A variable named averagePints of the data type Real initialized to 0
- A variable named highPints of the data type Real initialized to 0
- A variable named lowPints of the data type Real initialized to 0

```
Module main()
     //Declare local variables
     Declare String again = "no"

     _____

     _____

     _____

     _____

     _____

     While again == "no"
          //module calls below


          Display "Do you want to run again: yes or no"
          Input again
     End While
End Module
```

Step 2: Write a module call to a module named getPints that passes the pints array. Additionally, write a module header named getPints that accepts the pints array. (Reference Passing an Array as an Argument to a Function, p. 292.)

```
     //Module call
     Call _____ (_____)

     //Module header
     Module _____ (Real _____ [ ])
```

Step 3: Write a for loop that runs 7 times using the counter variable. Inside the for loop, allow the user to enter values into the array.
(Reference Using a Loop to Step Through an Array, p. 274.)

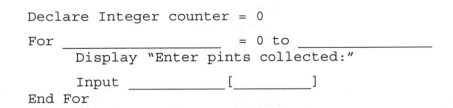

```
        Declare Integer counter = 0

        For _____ = 0 to _____
                Display "Enter pints collected:"

                Input _____[_____]
        End For
```

Step 4: Write a function call to a module named getTotal that passes the pints array and the totalPints variable. Additionally, write a function header named getTotal that accepts the pints array and the totalPints variable.

```
    //Function call
    totalPints = _____(_____, _____)

    //Function header
    Function _____(Real _____[ ], Real _____)
```

Step 5: Write a for loop that runs seven times using the counter variable. Inside the for loop, total up the values of the array and store in the variable totalPints. Also, return the correct variable from the function.
(Reference Totaling the Values in an Array, p. 286.)

```
    Declare Integer counter = 0
    Set totalPints = 0

    For _____ = 0 to _____

        Set _____ = _____ + _____[_____]
    End For

    Return _____
```

Step 6: Write a function call to a module named getAverage that passes the totalPints variable and the averagePints variable. Additionally, write a function header named getAverage that accepts the totalPints variable and the averagePints variable.

```
    //Function call
    averagePints = _____(_____, _____)

    //Function header
    Function _____(Real _____, Real _____)
```

Step 7: Write a statement that will calculate the average pints donated over the drive period. Also, return the correct variable from the function.
(Reference Averaging the Values in an Array, p. 287.)

```
averagePints = _____ / _____

Return _____
```

Step 8: Write a function call to a module named getHigh that passes the highPints variable and the pints array. Additionally, write a function header named getHigh that accepts the highPints variable and the pints array.

```
//Function call
highPints = _____ (_____ , _____ )

//Function header
Function _____(Real _____ , Real _____[ ])
```

Step 9: Write the code that will determine the highest value in an array. Also, return the correct variable from the function.
(Reference Finding the Highest Value in an Array, p. 288.)

```
Set highPints = pints[_____]
Set index = 1
For index = 1 to 6
      If _____[_____] > highPints Then
            Set _____ = _____[_____]
      End If
End For

Return _____
```

Step 10: Write a function call to a module named getLow that passes the lowPints variable and the pints array. Additionally, write a function header named getLow that accepts the lowPints variable and the pints array.

```
//Function call
lowPints = _____ (_____ , _____ )

//Function header
Function _____(Real _____ , Real _____[ ])
```

Step 11: Write the code that will determine the highest value in an array. Also, return the correct variable from the function.
(Reference Finding the Lowest Value in an Array, p. 290.)

```
Set lowPints = pints[_____]
Set index = 1
For index = 1 to 6
        If _____[_____] < lowPints Then
                Set _____ = _____[_____]
        End If
End For

Return _____
```

Step 12: Write a module call to a module named `displayInfo`. Pass the variables to the function that are needed to display the averagePints, the highPints, and the lowPints. Also, the module header that accepts the same variables.

```
//Module call
Call _____ (_____, _____, _____)
//Module header
Module _____(Real _____, Real _____, Real _____)
```

Name: _____

Lab 9.2 – Checking the Work

Using the program from Lab 9.1, complete the following checks for a better understanding of your work.

Step 1: Suppose the following number of pints were entered into the array.

Element	34	39	25	18	43	31	12
Index	0	1	2	3	4	5	6

Step 2: Recall Step 5 of Lab 9.1 that accumulates the pints collected.

```
Declare Integer counter = 0
Set totalPints = 0
For counter  = 0 to 6
     Set totalPints = totalPints + pints[counter]
End For
```

Step 3: Complete the following chart by writing what the counter and the totalPints value store on each iteration of the loop.

counter	totalPints
0	34
1	73
2	

Step 4: Recall Step 9 from Lab 9.1 that determines the high value.

```
Set highPints = pints[0]
Set index = 1
For index = 1 to 6
     If pints[index] > highPints Then
          Set highPints = pints[index]
     End If
End For
```

Step 5: Complete the following chart by writing what the highPints and the pints array values store on each iteration of the loop. Also conclude whether it will be True or False.

Pints	highPints	True or False
39	34	TRUE
25	39	FALSE
18		

Step 6: Recall Step 11 from Lab 9.1 that determines the low value.

```
Set lowPints = pints[0]
Set index = 1
For index = 1 to 6
    If pints[index] < lowPints Then
         Set lowPints = pints[index]
    End If
End For
```

Step 7: Complete the following chart by writing what the lowPints and the pints array values store on each iteration of the loop. Also conclude whether it will be True or False.

Pints	lowPints	True or False
39	34	FALSE
25	34	TRUE
18	25	

Name: _____

Lab 9.3 – Arrays and Flowcharts

Critical Review

Arrays in Raptor are defined as follows:

    arrayName[SIZE]

Size can either be a variable that is declared, or a specific number such as 10.

Array indices in Raptor start at 1. This is different than what is explained in the textbook, and also in Python.

This lab requires you to create a flowchart for the blood drive program in Lab 9.1. Use an application such as Raptor or Visio. These instructions assume you are using Raptor.

Step 1: Start Raptor and save your document as *Lab 9-3*. The *.rap* file extension will be added automatically.

Step 2: Start by adding a comment box with the necessary variables.

Step 3: Add your loop to run multiple times and your module calls in the main module.

Step 4: Add the getPints( ) module in main. Go to the getPints() module and add the following inside the module:

- An assignment statement that sets counter to 1. Remember, counter must be set to 1 because Raptor arrays must start at 1, not 0.
- A loop that runs as long as counter is less than 7. Remember, this should be written as counter > 7 because if yes, then the loop ends.
- An input statement that asks the user to enter number of pints, storing the answer in the array. The input should be entered as below.
- An assignment statement that will increment counter by 1.

Step 5: Add the getTotal( ) module in main. Go to the getTotal() module and add the following inside the module:

- Add an assignment statement that sets counter back to 1.
- Add an assignment statement that sets totalPints to 0.
- Add a loop that runs 7 times.
- Add an assignment statement that accumulates the value of the array. The input should be as below:
- Add an assignment statement that will increment counter by 1.

Step 6: Add the getAverage( ) module in main. Go to the getAverage() module and add the following inside the module:

- An assignment statement that sets counter back to 1.
- An assignment statement that sets averagePints to totalPints divided by 7.

Step 7: Add the getHigh( ) module in main. Go to the getHigh() module and add the following inside the module:

- An assignment statement that sets counter to 2. This refers to the second location in the array.
- An assignment statement that sets highPints to the 1 index of the pints array.
- A loop that iterates 7 times.
- Inside the loop, add a selection statement that determines if pints in the counter location is greater than highPints.
- If that is true, then set highPints to pints in the counter location.
- Increment counter by 1.

Step 8: Add the getLow( ) module in main. Go to the getLow() module and add the following inside the module:

- An assignment statement that sets counter to 2. This refers to the second location in the array.
- An assignment statement that sets lowPints to the 1 index of the pints array.
- Add a loop that iterates 7 times.
- Inside the loop, add a selection statement that determines if pints in the counter location is less than lowPints.
- If that is true, then set lowPints to pints in the counter location.
- Increment counter by 1.

Step 9: Add the displayInfo( ) module in main. Go to the display() module and add the following inside the module:

- Display the averagePints variable
- Display the highPints variable
- Display the lowPints variable

Step 10: Using the following input values, check your results. If there are errors, verify steps 1 through 10.

Element	34	39	25	18	43	31	12

Output should be as follows:

> The average pints collected: 28.8571
> The highest amount was: 43
> The lowest amount was: 12

Step 11: Copy your finished flowchart into a Word document; save and print.

Name: _____

Lab 9.4 – Arrays and Python Code

Critical Review

In Python, arrays are native objects called **lists**. List index starts at 0 (unlike Raptor).

The following is a method used when you know the elements of the array.

```
even_numbers = [2, 4, 6, 8, 10]
```

You can use the `print` statement to display an entire list, as shown here:

```
print even_numbers
```

Use the following method when you do not know what the elements should be, but you know the size:

```
numbers = [0] * 5
```

A loop can also be used to print the elements of the array. An example:

```
#A for in loop
for n in numbers:
    print n

#A while loop
    index = 0
while index < 5:
    print numbers [index]
    index = index + 1
```

The goal of this lab is to convert the blood drive program from Lab 9.1 to Python code.

Step 1: Start the IDLE Environment for Python. Prior to entering code, save your file by clicking on File and then Save. Select your location and save this file as *Lab9-4.py*. Be sure to include the .py extension.

Step 2: Document the first few lines of your program to include your name, the date, and a brief description of what the program does.

Step 3: Start your program with the following code for main:

```
#Lab 9-4 Blood Drive

    #the main function
    def main():
      endProgram = 'no'
      print
      while endProgram == 'no':
        print
        # declare variables


        # function calls


      endProgram = raw_input('Do you want to end program?
(Enter no or yes): ')
      while not (endProgram == 'yes' or endProgram == 'no'):
        print 'Please enter a yes or no'
        endProgram = raw_input('Do you want to end
program? (Enter no or yes): ')

    #the getPints function

    #the getTotal function

    #the getAverage function

    #the getHigh function

    #the getLow function

    #the displayInfo function

    # calls main
    main()
```

Step 4: Under the documentation for declaring variables, declare your variables and initialize them to 0. The array/list should be declared as follows:

```
    pints = [0] * 7
```

Step 5: Write a function call to the getPints function and pass it pints. The function will return pints, so set it equal to the function call. This should be done as follows:

```
    pints = getPints(pints)
```

Step 6: Under the documentation for the getPints function, write a while or a for in loop that will allow the user to enter pints into the array. This function might be written as follows.

```
#the getPints function
def getPints(pints):
  counter = 0
  while counter < 7:
      pints[counter] = input('Enter pints collected: ')
      counter = counter + 1
  return pints
```

Step 7: Write a function call to the getTotal function and pass it pints and totalPints. This function should be set to the totalPints variable since it will be returned from the function. The call might look as follows:

```
totalPints = getTotal(pints, totalPints)
```

Step 8: Under the documentation for the getTotal function, add the following statements:
- Initialize counter back to 0
- Add a while loop that runs 7 iterations and includes:
  - Accumulate totalPints by setting totalPints = totalPints + pints[counter]
  - Increment counter
- Return totalPints

Step 9: Write a function call to the getAverage function and pass it totalPints and averagePints. This function should be set to the averagePints variable since it will be returned from the function. The call might look like this:

```
averagePints = getAverage(totalPints, averagePints)
```

Step 10: Under the documentation for the getAverage function, add the following statements:
- A statement that will calculate averagePints as totalPints / 7
- Return averagePints

Step 11: Write a function call to the getHigh function and pass it pints and highPints. This function should be set to the highPints variable since it will be returned from the function. The call might look as follows:

```
highPints = getHigh(pints, highPints)
```

Step 12: Under the documentation for the getHigh function, add the following statements:

- Initialize highPints to pints[0]
- Set counter to 1
- Write a while loop that runs 7 iterations and includes:
  - An if statement that checks to see if pints[counter] > highPints
    - If it is true, set highPints to pints[counter]
  - Increment counter by 1
- Return highPints
- Be careful to watch your indentation on this function.

Step 13: Write a function call to the getLow function and pass it pints and lowPints. This function should be set to the lowPints variable since it will be returned from the function. The call might look as follows:

```
lowPints = getLow(pints, lowPints)
```

Step 14: Under the documentation for the getLow function, add the following statements:

- Initialize lowPints to pints[0]
- Set counter to 1
- Write a while loop that runs 7 iterations and includes:
  - An if statement that checks to see if pints[counter] < lowPints
    - If it is true, set lowPints to pints[counter]
  - Increment counter by 1
- Return lowPints
- Be careful to watch your indentation on this function.

Step 15: Write a function call to the displayInfo function and pass it averagePints, highPints, and lowPints.

Step 16: Under the documentation for the displayInfo function, write the statements that will display:
- the average pints donated
- the highest number of pints donated
- the lowest number of pints donated

Step 17: Run your program and check against the following output. If there are errors, go back through the steps to troubleshoot.

```
Enter pints collected: 43
Enter pints collected: 25
Enter pints collected: 64
Enter pints collected: 35
Enter pints collected: 19
Enter pints collected: 37
Enter pints collected: 46
The average number of pints donated is 38.4285714286
The highest pints donated is 64
The lowest pints donated is 19
```

Do you want to end program? (Enter no or yes): yes

Step 18: Execute your program so that it works. When your Python code is complete and correct, copy and paste your work into a Word document. Save and print your document, then turn it in for grading.

Name: _____

Lab 9.5 – Programming Challenge 1: Going Green

For the following programming problem, write:
1. the algorithm
2. the pseudocode
3. the flowchart
4. Python code

Copy and paste your work into a Word document, labeling each section. Save and print your document, then turn it in for grading.

Going Green

Last year, a local college implemented rooftop gardens as a way to promote energy efficiency and save money. Write a program that will allow the user to enter the energy bills from January to December for the year prior to going green. Next, allow the user to enter the energy bills from January to December of the past year after going green. The program should calculate the energy difference between the two years and display the two years' worth of data, along with the savings.

Hints: Create three arrays of size 12 each. The first array will store the first year of energy costs, the second array will store the second year after going green, and the third array will store the difference. Also, create a string array that stores the month names. These variables might be defined as follows:

```
notGreenCost = [0] * 12
goneGreenCost = [0] * 12
savings = [0] * 12
months = ['January', 'February', 'March', 'April',
'May', 'June', 'July', 'August', 'September', 'October',
'November', 'December']
```

Your sample output might look as follows:

```
Enter NOT GREEN energy costs for January
Enter now -->789
Enter NOT GREEN energy costs for February
Enter now -->790
Enter NOT GREEN energy costs for March
Enter now -->890
Enter NOT GREEN energy costs for April
Enter now -->773
Enter NOT GREEN energy costs for May
```

```
Enter now -->723
Enter NOT GREEN energy costs for June
Enter now -->759
Enter NOT GREEN energy costs for July
Enter now -->690
Enter NOT GREEN energy costs for August
Enter now -->681
Enter NOT GREEN energy costs for September
Enter now -->782
Enter NOT GREEN energy costs for October
Enter now -->791
Enter NOT GREEN energy costs for November
Enter now -->898
Enter NOT GREEN energy costs for December
Enter now -->923
--------------------------------------------------


Enter GONE GREEN energy costs for January
Enter now -->546
Enter GONE GREEN energy costs for February
Enter now -->536
Enter GONE GREEN energy costs for March
Enter now -->519
Enter GONE GREEN energy costs for April
Enter now -->493
Enter GONE GREEN energy costs for May
Enter now -->472
Enter GONE GREEN energy costs for June
Enter now -->432
Enter GONE GREEN energy costs for July
Enter now -->347
Enter GONE GREEN energy costs for August
Enter now -->318
Enter GONE GREEN energy costs for September
Enter now -->453
Enter GONE GREEN energy costs for October
Enter now -->489
Enter GONE GREEN energy costs for November
Enter now -->439
Enter GONE GREEN energy costs for December
Enter now -->516


--------------------------------------------------
```

SAVINGS

SAVINGS	NOT GREEN	GONE GREEN	MONTH
$ 243	$ 789	$ 546	January
$ 254	$ 790	$ 536	February
$ 371	$ 890	$ 519	March
$ 280	$ 773	$ 493	April
$ 251	$ 723	$ 472	May
$ 327	$ 759	$ 432	June
$ 343	$ 690	$ 347	July
$ 363	$ 681	$ 318	August
$ 329	$ 782	$ 453	September
$ 302	$ 791	$ 489	October
$ 459	$ 898	$ 439	November
$ 407	$ 923	$ 516	December

Do you want to end program? (Enter no or yes): yes

Lab 10: File Access

This lab accompanies Chapter 10 of *Starting Out with Programming Logic & Design*.

Name: _____

Lab 10.1 – File Access and Pseudocode

Critical Review

When a program needs to save data for later use, it writes the data in a file. You must do three things in order to work with a file:
1. Open the file.
2. Process the file.
3. Close the file.

An internal file must be created for an output file or input file, such as:

```
Declare OutputFile myFile   //to write out
Declare InputFile myFile    //to read in
```

A data file must also be created to store the output, such as:

```
Open myFile "thedata.txt"
```

New keywords and syntax include the following:

```
Open [InternalName] [FileName]
Write [InternalName] [String or Data]
Read [InternalName] [Data]
Close [InternalName]
AppendMode  //used with Open when need to append
```

Loops are used to process the data in a file. For example:

```
For counter = 1 to 5
   Display "Enter a number:"
   Input number
   Write myFile number
End For
```

When you need to read information from a file and don't known how many items there are, use the eof (end of file) function. For example:

```
While NOT eof(myFile)
   Read myFile number
   Display number
End While
```

This lab examines how to work with a file by writing pseudocode. Read the following problem prior to completing the lab. The program from Lab 9.1 will be used, with some modifications.

> The American Red Cross wants you to write a program that will calculate the average pints of blood donated during a blood drive. The program should take in the number of pints donated, based on a seven-hour drive period. The average pints donated during that period should be calculated and written to a file. Write a loop around the program to run multiple times. The data should be appended to the file to keep track of multiple days. If the user wants to print data from the file, read it in and then display it. Store the pints per hour and the average pints donated in a file called blood.txt.

Step 1: Note that the getPints, getTotal, and getAverage functions do not change. Also note that the references to displayInfo, getHigh, and getLow functions are removed to meet the new requirements. In the pseudocode below, add the following:

In the Main Module:
    a. Add a variable named option of the data type Integer.
    b. Input option.
    c. Write an if statement that will determine which option to run.
    d. Call a module called writeToFile that passes pints and averagePints.
    e. Call a module called readFromFile that passes pints and averagePints.

In the writeToFile Module:
    f. Declare an output file called outFile in AppendMode with the name bloodFile. (Reference Appending Data to an Existing File, p. 370.)
    g. Open the internal file (bloodFile) and a text file named blood.txt. (Reference Creating a File and Writing Data to It, p. 362.)
    h. Write the string "Pints Each Hour" to the file. (Reference Writing Data to a File, p. 363.)
    i. In the while loop, write each element of the pints array to the bloodFile. (Reference Using Loops to Process Files, p. 371.)
    j. Write the string "Average Pints" to the file.
    k. Write the value of averagePints to the file.
    l. Close the bloodFile. (Reference Closing an Output File, p. 363.)

In the readFromFile Module:
    m. Declare an input file called inFile with the name bloodFile. (Reference Reading Data from a File, p. 366.)

n. Open the internal file (bloodFile) and a text file named blood.txt.
o. Read the string "Pints Each Hour" in from your file and store into a variable str1. This should be done as Read bloodFile str1. The string will be stored in the variable str1.
p. Display str1 to the screen.
q. Read pints in from the bloodFile and store in the pints array.
r. Display pints to the screen.
s. Read the string "Average Pints" in from your file and store into a variable str2.
t. Display str2 to the screen.
u. Read averagePints in from the bloodFile.
v. Display averagePints to the screen
w. Close the file. (Reference Closing an Input File, p. 367.)

```
Module main()
      //Declare local variables
      Declare String again = "no"
      Declare Real pints[7]
      Declare Real totalPints
      Declare Real averagePints

      a. _____

      While again == "no"
            //module calls below
            Display "Enter 1 to enter in new data and
store to file"
            Display "Enter 2 to display data from the
file"

      Input b. _____


            c. If _____ == _____
Then
                  Call getPints(pints)
                  Call getTotal(pints, totalPints)
                  Call getAverage(totalPints,
averagePints)
                  d. Call
_____(_____,_____)
            Else
                  e. Call
_____(_____,_____)
            End If
```

```
                    Display "Do you want to run again: yes or no"
                    Input again
            End While
End Module

Module getPints(Real pints[])
        Declare Integer counter = 0
        For counter  = 0 to 6
                Display "Enter pints collected:"
                Input pints[counter]
        End For
End Module

Function getTotal(Real pints[], Real totalPints)
        Declare Integer counter = 0
        Set totalPints = 0
        For counter = 0 to 6
                Set totalPints = totalPints + pints[counter]
                End For
Return totalPints

Function getAverage(Real totalPints, Real averagePints)
        averagePints = totalPints / 7
Return averagePints

Module writeToFile(Real pints[], Real averagePints)
```

f. Declare _____ _____ _____

g. Open _____ _____

h. Write _____ "_____"

Declare Integer counter = 0

i. While counter < 7

    Write _____ _____[_____]

    Set counter = counter + 1

End While

j. Write _____ "_____"

k. Write _____ _____

l. Close _____

```
End Module

Module readFromFile(Real pints[], Real averagePints)
```

m. Declare _____ _____

n. Open _____ "_____"

o. Read _____ _____

p. Display _____

q. Read _____ _____

r. Display _____

s. Read _____ _____

t. Display _____

u. Read _____ _____

v. Display _____

w. Close _____

End Module

Name: _____

Lab 10.2 – File Access and Flowcharts

Critical Review

Output to a File using Raptor

The Output symbol is used to output data to a text file. When an Output symbol is reached during Raptor program execution, the system determines whether or not output has been *redirected.*

- If output *has* been redirected, meaning an output file has been specified, the output is written to the specified file.
- If output has *not* been redirected, it goes to the Master Console.

One way to redirect output to a file is by creating a call symbol and adding the following:

```
Redirect_Output("file.txt")
```

Note: If the file specified already exists, it will be overwritten with no warning! All of the file's previous contents will be lost!

The second version of Redirect_Output redirects output with a simple yes or true argument:

```
Redirect_Output(True)
```

This delays the selection of the output file to run time. When the Call symbol containing Redirect_Output is executed, a file selection dialog box will open, and the user can specify which file is to be used for output.

After a successful call to Redirect_Output, the program writes its output to the specified file. To reset Raptor so that subsequent Output symbols write their output to the Master Console, another call to Redirect_Output is used, this time with a False (No) argument:

```
Redirect_Output(False)
```

After this call is executed, the output file is closed, and subsequent outputs will again go to the Master Console. There is no Append option in Raptor.

Input to a File using Raptor

This is done the same way, except `Redirect_Input( )` is called. To pull something in from a file, use the input symbols.

This lab requires you to create a flowchart for the blood drive program in Lab 10.1. Use an application such as Raptor or Visio. These instructors assume you use Raptor.

Step 1: Start Raptor and open your *Lab 9-3*. Save this file as *Lab 10-3*. The *.rap* file extension will be added automatically.

Step 2: Remove the references you no longer need: the `highPints` and `lowPints` variables, and the `getHigh`, `getLow`, and `displayInfo` modules. With the modules, first delete the function calls, and then right-click on the tabs and select Delete Subchart.

Step 3: In main after the module call to `getAverage`, add a call to `writeToFile`.

Step 4: Go to that module and add a call symbol. Add the following: `Redirect_Output("blood1.txt".)`

Step 5: Add an output symbol that prints the string "`Pints Each Hour`".

Step 6: Add an assignment symbol that sets `counter` to 1.

Step 7: Add a loop symbol that has the condition of `counter > 7`.

Step 8: If the condition is `False`, add an output symbol that prints `pints[counter]` to the file. This should look as follows:

Step 9: Add an assignment statement that increments counter by 1.

Step 10: If the condition is true, add an output symbol that prints the string "Average Pints" to the file.

Step 11: Add an output symbol that prints averagePints to the file.

Step 12: Add a call symbol that closes the file. This should look as follows:

Step 13: In main after the call to writeToFile, add a call to readFromFile.

Step 14: In the readFromFile module, add a call symbol to Redirect_Input, such as Redirect_Input("blood1.txt".)

Step 15: Add an Input symbol that gets str1. This should look as follows:

Step 16: Add an assignment statement that sets `counter` to 1.

Step 17: Add a loop statement. If the loop is `False`, get the next value from the file and store it in `pints[counter]`. This should look as follows:

Step 18: Increment `counter` by 1.

Step 19: If the loop is `True`, get `str2` with an input symbol.

Step 20: Add an input symbol that gets `averagePints`.

Step 21: Add a call symbol that sets `Redirect_Input` to `True`.

Step 22: In the Main module, add an input symbol under the loop symbol. This should ask the user to enter 1 if they want to take in data and add to the file or 2 if they want to print information from the file. Store this in a variable called `option`.

Step 23: Add a decision symbol that asks if `option` is equal to 1. If it is, call the `getPints`, `getTotal`, `getAverage`, and `writeToFile` module. If it is not, call the `readFromFile` module.

Step 24: Run your program once and be sure to select option 1 on the first time through. This will create a file called `blood1.txt` in your directory where your Raptor flowchart is located. An example file might contain the following:

```
Pints Each Hour
45
34
```

```
23
54
34
23
34
Average Pints
35.2857
```

Step 25: Go to your file called `blood1.txt` and examine the contents. Print out the file.

Step 26: Run your program again, but select option 2. You can test to see if it is reading values properly into your program by examining the contents of the variables that are listed on the left. The following is an example:

```
AVERAGEPINTS: 35.2857
COUNTER: 8
ENDPROGRAM: "yes"
OPTION: 2
PINTS[]
    Size: 7
    <1>: 45
    <2>: 34
    <3>: 23
    <4>: 54
    <5>: 34
    <6>: 23
    <7>: 34
STR1: "Pints Each Hour"
STR2: "Average Pints"
```

Step 27: Paste your finished flowchart into a Word document. Save and print.

Name: _____

Lab 10.3 – File Access and Python Code

Critical Review

Writing to a File

When writing to a file, you must create an internal file name such as outFile.

This file must then be opened using two arguments. The first argument is the name of the file and the second is the mode you want to open the file in. You can select either the 'a' append mode or the 'w' write mode. For example:

```
outFile = open('filename.txt', 'w')
```

A string literal can be written to a file like this:
```
Print >> outFile, 'Header Information'
```

Variables must be converted to strings as they are written to a file and a call to write must occur. Additionally, a '\n' can be appended to cause a return statement in your file. For example:
```
outFile.write(str(variableName) + '\n')
```

Arrays are written to a file using a loop. For example:
```
counter = 0
while counter < 7:
    outFile.write(str(arrayName[counter]) + '\n')
    counter = counter + 1
```

Files must then be closed. This works the same for both input and output.
```
outFile.close()    or    inFile.close()
```

Reading from a File

When reading from a file, you must create an internal file name such as inFile.

This file must then be opened using two arguments. The first argument is the name of the file and the second is the mode you want to open the file in, in this case, 'r' for read. For example:
```
inFile = open('filename.txt', 'r')
```

Reading from a file is done sequentially in this lab, and a call to read must occur. If a string header is done first, that must be read into a string variable. That variable can then be used for processing within the program.

A string literal can be read from a file and displayed to the screen, such as:
```
str1 = inFile.read()
print str1
```

Arrays and variables can be read as a single input like this:
```
arrayName = inFile.read()
print arrayName
```

183

The goal of this lab is to convert the blood drive program from Lab 10.1 to Python code.

Step 1: Start the IDLE Environment for Python. Prior to entering code, save your file by clicking on File and then Save. Select your location and save this file as *Lab*10-3.*py*. Be sure to include the .py extension.

Step 2: Document the first few lines of your program to include your name, the date, and a brief description of what the program does.

Step 3: Start your program with the following code:

```
#Lab 10-3 Blood Drive

#the main function
def main():
  endProgram = 'no'
  print
  while endProgram == 'no':
    option = 0
    print
    print 'Enter 1 to enter in new data and store to file'
    print 'Enter 2 to display data from the file'
    option = input('Enter now ->')
    print

    # declare variables
    pints = [0] * 7
    totalPints = 0
    averagePints = 0

    if option == 1:
      # function calls
      pints = getPints(pints)
      totalPints = getTotal(pints, totalPints)
      averagePints = getAverage(totalPints, averagePints)

    else:


    endProgram = raw_input('Do you want to end program?
(Enter no or yes): ')
    while not (endProgram == 'yes' or endProgram == 'no'):
      print 'Please enter a yes or no'
      endProgram = raw_input('Do you want to end
program? (Enter no or yes): ')
```

```
#the getPints function
def getPints(pints):
  counter = 0
  while counter < 7:
      pints[counter] = input('Enter pints collected: ')
      counter = counter + 1
  return pints

#the getTotal function
def getTotal(pints, totalPints):
  counter = 0
  while counter < 7:
    totalPints = totalPints + pints[counter]
    counter = counter + 1
  return totalPints

#the getAverage function
def getAverage(totalPints, averagePints):
  averagePints = float(totalPints) / 7
  return averagePints

#the writeToFile function
def writeToFile(averagePints, pints):

#the readFromFile function
def readFromFile(averagePints, pints):

# calls main
main()
```

Step 4: Under option 1 in main, add a function call to `writeToFile` and pass it `averagePints` and `pints`. This should be done after the other calls. This should look as follows:

```
writeToFile(averagePints, pints)
```

Step 5: Under option 2 in main, add a function call to `readFromFile` and pass it `averagePints` and `pints`. This should be done after the other calls. This should look as follows:
```
readFromFile(averagePints, pints)
```

Step 6: Under the documentation and the function header for the `writeToFile` function, create an `outFile` and call the `open` function. Pass this function the name of the text file and open it in append mode. This should look like this:

```
outFile = open('blood.txt', 'a')
```

Step 7: The next step is to write the string 'Pints Each Hour' to the file:

```
print >> outFile, 'Pints Each Hour'
```

Step 8: Initial counter to 0 and add a while loop with the condition of counter < 7. Inside the while loop, write the value of the array pints to the file. This should look as follows:

```
outFile.write(str(pints[counter]) + '\n')
counter = counter + 1
```

Step 9: Outside of the while loop, write the string 'Average Pints' to the file.

Step 10: Next, write the averagePints variable to the file. This should look as follows:

```
outFile.write(str(averagePints) + '\n\n')
```

Step 11: The last item in this function is to close the outFile:

```
outFile.close()
```

Step 12: Under the documentation and the function header for the readFromFile function, create an inFile and call the open function. Pass this function the name of the text file and open it in read mode. This should look as follows:

```
inFile = open('blood.txt', 'r')
```

Step 13: Next, read in the string 'Pints Each Hour' and print this to the screen:

```
str1 = inFile.read()
print str1
```

Step 14: Read in the pints array as an entire list and print this to the screen. This is done as follows:

```
pints = inFile.read()
print pints
print  #adds a blank line
```

Step 15: Read in the string 'Average Pints' and print this to the screen.

Step 16: Read in averagePints and print this to the screen.

Step 17: Close the inFile.

Step 18: Run your program and for the first execution, select option 1. Run the program more than once and enter at least 2 sets of data. The append mode should keep track of everything. The contents of your file will be stored in the same directory that your Python code is in. Print out the contents of the file.

Step 19: Run your program again and select option 2 on the first iteration. This should display to the screen information that is stored in your file.

Step 20: Execute your program so that it works. When your Python code is complete and correct, copy and paste your work into a Word document. Save and print your document, then turn it in for grading.

Name: _____

Lab 10.4 – Programming Challenge 1: Going Green and File Interaction

For the following programming problem from Lab 9.5, write:
1. the algorithm
2. the pseudocode
3. the flowchart
4. Python code

Note that the in addition to what the program already does, it should create a file called savings.txt and store the savings array to a file. This should be done in append mode in Python and your pseudocode, but not in Raptor as it is not an option.

Going Green and File Interaction

Last year, a local college implemented rooftop gardens as a way to promote energy efficiency and save money. Write a program that will allow the user to enter the energy bills from January to December for the year prior to going green. Next, allow the user to enter the energy bills from January to December of the past year after going green. The program should calculate the energy difference from the two years and display the two years worth of data, along with the savings. Additionally, the savings array should be printed to a file called savings.txt.